Portraits

of

Temperament

David

Keirsey

Copyright © 1987

Prometheus Nemesis Book Company
Post Office Box 2748, Del Mar, CA 92014

Second edition, 1988

Third edition, 1995

Contents

Introduction

If I seem out of step with you I ask you only to wonder about me, nothing more.

If my beliefs, my aims, and my feelings are different from yours, this gives you no warrant to put me down or to try to change me in your own image. Does it not take all kinds to make the world go round?

If, on the other hand, I am just like you, then we both may rejoice in our similitude, and communicate without let. But should we not also rejoice that others are not like us?

How dull that we would all be the same. And how fruitless.

When we marry, the license we are given is not to reshape our mate after ourselves. Should we succeed in our Pygmalion project we must thereupon abandon our remodeled mate and seek another, more attractive. For are we not attracted to our complement, precisely in the degree our prospective mate completes us?

When we beget offspring and observe that they seem to take more after our mate than ourselves, does this waywardness of development give us license to sculpt them in our own image? Is not one of us enough?

Differences can be for our enjoyment and our appreciation.

But most of all for our self-understanding. We can know what we are only insofar as we know what we are not. A prophet said:

> Send not to know for whom the bell tolls.
> It tolls for you, for you are involved with mankind.

This is a book of portraits. Eight of them. Perhaps you are one of these eight kinds of people. Perhaps your spouse, your child, your parent, your boss, your employee, maybe even your enemy is herein portrayed. Would it not be useful to compare these people with yourself?

For you who would go directly to your portrait and skip the rest, you might complete the questionnaire in Appendix A and then find the pertinent portrayal. Then, you may find some of the other portraits interesting to contrast with yours.

For you who want a rationale before looking at the portraits, the History and Overview will give you that. After reading the History and Overview, if you are still interested, you might complete the questionnaire in Appendix A to determine what portrait pertains to you. After that, it may be useful to you to read the other portraits to define what you are not.

For you who prefer to look at all the portraits to decide which, if any, portrays you, you need not bother with either the History and Overview or with the questionnaire in Appendix A.

The point is that this book need not be read from beginning to end or in any particular order. People are different in how they read books too.

History and Overview

We have long argued about origins. Since organisms can be dissected into organs, organs seen as cellular, and cells seen as complex, some of us have concluded that organisms are integrations of parts. Just as machines are constituted of parts, so then are organisms. This belief survives even though organisms are *observably* whole and integrated from the very beginning and are *never* otherwise. The embryo is as organized and whole as the old man. *Seeing* that organisms come from other organisms, already whole, already integrated, some of us believe organisms never become an integration of parts. Organisms cannot *become* integrated because they started out that way. Those who think wholes are integrations of parts—the partists—are interested in explaining how *wholes* originate. Those who think parts are differentiations of wholes—the wholists—are interested in explaining how *parts* originate. This ancient dispute cannot be settled because the two sides are not concerned with the same problem.

In the inorganic sciences the wholists, now called systemists, were dominant during the 20th century and produced impressive technological advances, such as the atomic bomb, nuclear generators, rocket propulsion, and the computer. In the organic sciences the partists, now called elementists, were dominant in the 20th century, such that the progress made by a few wholists was ignored.

The shadow cast over the organic sciences was very dark, expecially in the case of anthropology, communications, psychiatry, psychology, psychopathology, and sociology. In each of these sciences the elementists developed a vocabulary of element analogies in their attempts to explain behavior and published countless books and articles employing this vocabulary. For example, in psychopathology, Freud invented many imaginary elements, such as the Ego, Id, Superego, Psychic Sensor, Libido, and Unconscious, and speculated on how these imaginary elements functioned. Thus to give his imaginary elements something to do he invented corresponding imaginary functions. What is the Ego? It is at once a chamber to hold mechanisms inside and an integrator of these mechanisms. At the time all Freud had as model for his analogies was the hydraulic machine, though telephone and phonograph were soon to appear. So he said that mind both is structured like and functions like such a machine. Another example, Hubbard,[1] would later say that mind is a tape recorder, and Berne would invoke the metaphor of the hydraulic machine governed by an electronic servomechanism. And there are now numerous documents written by psychologists depicting mind as a computer. Thus each elementist looks to the machines of his time for analogies of mind, will, and soul. But the systemists

---

[1] See *Dianetics*. This book was published in 1950 and had sold millions of copies by 1987. Also the practice of 'erasing bad tapes in the mind' was institutionalized as a church with thousands of 'healers' making a living in the business of erasing bad tapes. Not too bad a track record for a science fiction writer! The point not to miss is that Hubbard's analogies are no more far-fetched than those of many elementist cults in psychology, psychopathology, and psychiatry. Each rests its case with machine analogies.

turned to analogies too, since they, like the elementists, had no choice in the matter.

SelfActualization.   The point is that when trying to give an account of what cannot be observed we are all confined to analogies, that is, to similes and metaphors. Unable to describe what cannot be visualized, the mind for instance, elementists have said mind is a closed chamber, with tubes and wires connecting it to other chambers. Thus mind could be visualized easily. The systemists, confined as were elementists to analogies, developed their own vocabulary of analogies. But these analogies differed in a very important way. Instead of describing imaginary actions in terms of visible machines, the systemists likened them to visible organic changes. For example, Köhler[2] said behavior 'unfolds' like a flower, calling this the principle of self-distribution. Another systemist, Wheeler[3], said the mature organism acts as a goal for the immature organism—the acorn 'tries' to become an oak tree, the principle of closure. So the systemists developed what they called principles of self-actualization—self-development and self-regulation. *The organism develops and regulates itself.*

Where the elementists used *thing* analogies, the systemists used *change* analogies. For example, Freud likened the Unconscious to a pressure chamber and Jung likened the Archetypes to nodes of energy in such a pressure chamber. In contrast von Ehrenfels likened physiology to a melody and Rubin likened the organism-environment relation to the figure-ground relation. While the elementists were concerned with how the organism is developed and regulated by *elements*, the systemists were concerned with how the

---

[2] See *Gestalt Psychology.*

[3] See *The Laws of Human Nature* and *The Principles of Mental Development.*

organism developed and regulated *itself*. The principles of the two perspectives may be counterposed:

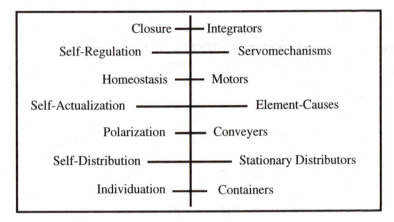

History of the System Analogies

Over two thousand years ago in Greece, Hippocrates wrote of four types of temperament: Sanguines (cheerful and optimistic), Melancholics (sad and pessimistic), Phlegmatic (calm and detached), and Choleric (passionate and enthusiastic). His contemporary, Plato, named four kinds of character to correspond with the temperaments of Hippocrates: Artists, Guardians, Scientists, and Philosophers. The idea of four kinds of personality has been used in Europe and America since Greek times and has reappeared in the 20th century in the works of several investigators:

Hippocrates -370	Sanguine	Melancholic	Phlegmatic	Choleric
Plato -340	Artisan	Guardian	Scientist	Philosopher
Paracelsus 1540	Salamander	Gnome	Sylph	Nymph
Adickes 1907	Innovative	Traditional	Agnostic	Dogmatic
Spränger 1914	Esthetic	Economic	Theoretical	Religious
Kretschmer 1920	Hyperesthetic	Anesthetic	Depressive	Hypomanic
Fromm 1947	Exploiting	Hoarding	Marketing	Receptive
Myers 1955	Perceptive	Judicious	Thoughtful	Feelingful
Keirsey 1978	Dionysian	Epimethean	Promethean	Apollonian

Early in the century Adickes indicated that his substitutes for the Platonic types, the "Agnostics" and "Dogmatics" share an "Autonomous" attitude, meaning that they are self-determining or self-guided, while the "Traditionals" and "Innovators" share a "Heteronomous" attitude, meaning that they are other-determined or other-guided people.

Not long after this, in renaming the Platonic personalities, Spränger pointed out that his "Religious" and "Economic" types share a "Social" attitude, meaning by this that they tend to put moral sanction above functional utility in determining how to procede toward a goal. He also said that his "Theoretical" and "Esthetic" types share a "Political" attitude, meaning that they are inclined to put functional utility ahead of moral sanction in implementing a goal. At mid-century Isabel Myers, taking her cue from Carl Jung, said that her "Feeling" and "Thinking" types are both "Intuitive" people, meaning that they are both abstract in attitude, while her "Perceptive" and "Judicious" types are both "Sensory" people, meaning that they are concrete in attitude. Thus the Platonic types can be arranged in accord with the social-political and intuitive-sensory dimensions:

	INTUITIVE	**SENSORY**
SOCIAL	PHILOSOPHERS	GUARDIANS
POLITICAL	SCIENTISTS	ARTISANS

It is remarkable that none of the investigators of the 20th century mentioned Plato or Hippocrates or Galen in their deliberations. Yet all of them came to similar conclusions regarding the structure of personality: we are born with out temperament and acquire our character as our inborn temperament interacts with our social environment. Let us examine the many names given the four kinds of personality in accord with the dimensions given by Spränger and Myers:

	INTUITIVE (Abstract)	SENSORY (Concrete)	Myers 1955
SOCIAL (Sanction)	Choleric	Melancholic	Hippocrates -370
	Philosopher	Guardian	Plato -340
	Nymphs	Gnomes	Paracelsus 1550
	Dogmatic	Traditional	Adickes 1907
	Religious	Economical	Spränger 1914
	Hyeresthetic	Depressive	Kretschmer 1920
	Receptive	Hoarding	Fromm 1947
	Feeling	Judging	Myers 1955
	Apollonian	Epimethean	Keirsey 1978
POLITICAL (Utility)	Phlegmatic	Sanguine	Hippocrates -370
	Scientist	Artisan	Plato -340
	Sylphs	Salamanders	Paracelsus 1550
	Agnostic	Innovative	Adickes 1907
	Theoretic	Aesthetic	Spränger 1914
	Anesthetic	Hypomanic	Kretschmer 1920
	Marketing	Exploiting	Fromm 1947
	Thinking	Perceiving	Myers 1955
	Promethean	Dionysian	Keirsey 1978

The Faculty Types of Isabel Myers. In mid-century Isabel Myers and her mother Catheryn Briggs devised the *Myers-Briggs Type Indicator*. It was a paper and pencil personality inventory designed to identify sixteen different types of personality. It gradually caught on, so that by the 90s it was far outselling all other such inventories. The astonishing increase in the use of the test around the world gave the quadratic analogy of behavior a powerful boost, so powerful, indeed, as to cause, inadvertently,[5] a world-wide resurgence of interest in the ancient ideology. This analogy challenged the widely held view that environment shapes our behavior, that we are but clay figures to be sculpted by the events in our lives.

Myers defined four kinds[6] of people, naming them Intuitive Feeling types, Intuitive Thinking types, Sensible Judging types, and Sensible Perceiving types. These four analogies corresponded closely to those defined earlier by Adickes, Spränger, Kretschmer, and Fromm. These follow:

The Sensible Perceiving Types (SP). According to Myers the Sense Perceptives (SPs) are adaptable, artistic, athletic, do not fight reality, don't get wrought up, are easy going, act with effortless economy, enjoy life, are gifted with machines and tools, are good natured, have no use for theories, know what's going on, look for workable compromises, notice reality, are open minded, persuasive,

---

[5] Myers attempted to implement the ideas of Carl Jung, but her common sense diverted her from some of his grossest errors, such that she captured the nature of the four temperaments in spite of Jung.

[6] Owing to an error inherited from Carl Jung, Myers misnamed the latter two kinds of people, and so improperly defined two of the variants of each. The "Sensible Introverts" should have been called the "Sensible Judges", thus including the 'extroverts' in the group, while the "Sensible Extroverts" should have been called the "Sensible Perceptors", thus including the 'introverts' in the group. With this correction, the Myers personality types become the Intuitive Feelers (NF), Intuitive Thinkers (NT), Sensible Judgers (SJ), and Sensible Perceptors (SP). It may be noted that these four terms are used throughout the book as column headings and therefore, combined with row numbers, become cell headings. Jung was a Swiss medic, also a contemporary and disciple of Freud, who wrote many volumns on pathology and healing. His book *Psychological Types* was an excursion from his main work, an excursion he said he did not take very seriously, nor did the Jungian "analysts" who were trained in Jungian ideology to perform "analytic psychotherapy".

remember reality, see needs of the moment, are sensitive to color, line, texture, store useful facts, are tolerant, unprejudiced, and want first-hand experiences. The core of this definition is the artistic-athletic-cheerful-mechanical-realistic pattern.[7]

The Sensible Judging Types (SJ). Myers portrayed the sensible judging (SJ) type as dependable, factual, painstaking, routinized, thorough, conservative, consistent, detailed, hard-working, patient, persevering, sensible, and stable. Moreover, she wrote, SJs are not impulsive or distractable, are good at maintenance, at citing cases, at meeting the visible needs of others. The core of this definition is the dependable-factual-painstaking-routinized-thorough pattern.[8] This pattern is unique and distinct, markedly different from the other patterns Myers portrayed.

The Intuitive Thinking Types (NT). Myers defines[9] the NT as abstract, analytic, complex, curious, efficient, exacting, impersonal, independent, ingenious, intellectual, inventive, logical, scientific, theoretical, research oriented, systematic. The core of this portrayal is the analytic-curious-efficient-inventive-logical pattern. The configuration is quite unique and very distinct, not overlapping in the least with the other three configurations she describes. Although Myers suggests that many of these traits apply to the sensible thinking types, the only ones applicable are exactitude

---

[7] See page A5 in *The Myers Briggs Type Indicator* (1962). It is true that Myers said this only of the extroverted SP, but it applies to the introverted SP equally well, the degree of gregariousness having nothing to do with the matter.

[8] See page A6 in *The Myers Briggs Type Indicator* (1962). It is true Myers attributed this pattern only to the introverted SJs, but the definition applies as well to the extroverted SJs, introversion and extroversion being unrelated to the definition.

[9] See page 56 in *The Myers Briggs Type Indicator* (1962).

and independence, exactitude in the case of SJs and independence in the case of SPs. Note, however, that none of the core traits apply to the sensible types.

The Intuitive Feeling Types (NF). According to Myers[1] the NF is enthusiastic, humane, religious, subjective, sympathetic, insightful, creative, imaginative, and does well as researcher, teacher, preacher, counselor, writer, psychologist, psychiatrist, and linguist. The nucleus of this portrayal lies in five of the traits: imaginative-sympathetic-linguistic-enthusiastic-subjective. Certainly this is a unique pattern and strikingly different from the other three patterns she defines. Not that others aren't or can't be sympathetic or enthused or subjective or imaginative or linguistically fluent—of course they can be—but no other type is all of these all the time. NFs are. The four configurations given by Myers add features to the Hippocratean temperament analogies hitherto unnoticed, besides being clear-cut and distinct from one another. These definitions may be arrayed in the quadratic matrix discussed above:

	INTUITIVE	SENSORY
SANCTIONING	feeling enthusiastic subjective sympathetic linguistic imaginative	judging thorough routinized dependable painstaking factual
UTILITARIAN	thinking analytic efficient curious inventive logical	perceiving artistic athletic cheerful mechanical realistic

[1] See page 56 in *The Myers Briggs Type Indicator* (1962).

Names for the Four Temperaments. What was I to call these four kinds of people? Should I use the words of Hippocrates, or of one of his followers? Or should I adopt terms of greater generality? After all, each set of terms given by Hippocrates, Plato, Paracelsus, Adickes, Spränger, Kretschmer, Fromm, Myers, and Keirsey deal with only one aspect of personality. To use any set is to give a slant to the definitions so named. The row and column headings of the quadratic matrix are the generic terms for naming the four types: Concrete Utilitarians, Concrete Sanctioners, Abstract Utilitarians, and Abstract Sanctioners. But these expressions are cumbersome and they do not lend themselves very well to imagery. What is needed are four words suggesting concreteness versus abstractness, on the one hand, and sanction versus utility, on the other. The following may be useful:

Concrete Utilitarians	=	Artisans
Concrete Sanctioners	=	Guardians
Abstract Utilitarians	=	Rationals
Abstract Sanctioners	=	Idealists

The Four Temperaments and Their Eight RoleMessage Forms

There are two variants of each of the four temperaments. Thus there are two different Artisans, two different Guardians, two different Rationals, two different Idealists. These variants are different from each other in the way they communicate about the *kind of relationship* they are willing to have with others. We are social creatures living in a social context. We necessarily play roles in relation to each other—husband to wife, parent to child, sibling to sibling, boss to subordinate, doctor to patient, teacher to learner. But we differ fundamentaly in how we play those roles and in how we let others know how we play those roles. We differ, in other words, in our *rolemessages*.

Directive RoleMessages. Some of us naturally and comfortably define the roles we and others are to play in relation to each other. For example, we might assume the role of teacher by instructing another on how to do something, thus defining our role as teacher and the other's role as learner. Or we might advise another on how to regain his or her health, thus defining our role as healer and the other's role as patient. But we may not be deliberate about this, that is, may not first decide to do it beforehand. We may just do it as a matter of course, and even be surprised to learn of this habit when someone points it out to us. In other words we can *spontaneously initiate role definitions*, can be prone to make the first move in defining the relationship we intend to have with others. Thus inclined, we may be referred to as *role proactive* or *role assertive* in that we cast ourselves and others into roles. In defining role relationships we usually speak in a commanding way, give orders, issue directives. Since our communications are more often than not directives rather than informatives, since we are natural directors of role relationships, it is fitting that our role defining messages be referred to as *'RoleDirectives'*.

Informative RoleMessages. Some of us, in contrast to those who traffic in roledirective messages, tend to wait for others to propose the role we are to play and then respond to that move by *informing* the RoleDirectors of our assent or dissent. For example, I might disclose that I have a headache, whereupon you may advise me to take some aspirin, and in so doing define the reciprocal roles as healer and patient. Whether I respond, "That's a good idea" or "Aspirin bothers my stomach," I have informed you of my acceptance or rejection of my assigned action in the role of patient, but I have not rejected your right to cast me into the role of patient. In other words I have responded to your initiative in such a manner as to confirm your right to define the relationship. Since I am informative rather than directive in regard to setting role relationships, my message may justly be called a *'roleinformative'*. So inclined, I would rarely speak in a commanding way, rarely give orders, rarely issue directives. When I do, it is with some discomfort and self-consciousness and my directives would usually be disqualified by apology. For instance, those who send roleinformatives are likely to ask for information even when the intent is to ask the other to do something—"Would you mind telling me the time?" or "What do you think about going to a movie tonight?" In contrast those who are prone to send roledirectives are likely to ask "What time is it?" or suggest "Let's go to a movie tonight." Roleinformatives can be said to be reactive rather than proactive, responsive rather than assertive.

Implicit and Explicit RoleDirectives.

It is true, of course, that all messages determine role relationships. When I tell you I have a headache I can be seen as having invited you to take the role of healer and to assign me the role of patient. But note carefully that by *informing* you of my headache my message has only *implied* that I am willing to be cast in the role of patient. I wait for you to assume the healing role and cast me in the patient role. Should your prescription, in my view, be ill advised, then I just might deny your right to take the role of healer. Note carefully that roleinformative messages only implicitly and hesitantly set roles, while roledirectives do so explicitly and unhesitantly.

Observability.

The degree in which people are roledirective or roleinformative in relation to others is quite observable, even more observable than the degree of abstractness or concreteness of communications, or the degree of cooperativeness or pragmatism. Not only is this difference more observable, it *may* be more important in determining whether a relationship is continued or discontinued, amicable or hostile, constructive or destructive.

Names for the Eight RoleMessaging Types. The same problems encountered in naming the four temperaments is once again faced in naming the eight rolemessage types. Only this time there are no words that have been used in the past to classify communications about roles. The Myers terminology—SPt, SPf, SJt, SJf, NTj, NTp, NFj, NFp —will not do, because the similarity between these definitions and the present ones is not great enough[11] to warrant one-to-one correspondence. The following names have been selected for their generality and imagery (the correlated Myers-Briggs terms are appended to indicate correlation):

Names of the Eight SubTypes

ArtisanRoleDirectors	=	Operators (SPt)
ArtisanRoleInformers	=	Players (SPf)
GuardianRoleDirectors	=	Monitors (SJt)
GuardianRoleInformers	=	Conservators (SJf)
RationalRoleDirectors	=	Organizers (NTj)
RationalRoleInformers	=	Engineers (NTp)
IdealistRoleDirectors	=	Mentors (NFj)
IdealistRoleInformers	=	Advocates (NFp)

Gregariousness. Each of us is in some degree gregarious. But some are more gregarious than others. Even so, our need to interact probably varies from hour to hour and day

---

[11] My guess is that the higher the J scores for Ns on the MBTI and Temperament Sorter, the higher the correlation with roledirectiveness. I also guess that the higher the T score for Ss on the MBTI and Sorter, the higher the correlation with roledirectiveness. Given high scores I estimate the index of correlation between the eight temperaments and type indication on the MBTI and Temperament Sorter to be about sixty percent (.6). Of course, there is no question of validity in tests such as the MBTI, Temperament Sorter, Grey-Wheelright, CPI, MMPI, and the like. Personality tests cannot be validated.

to day. Some of us probably become more extroverted as we grow older while others of us become less so over time and more and more retreat to private places. Sociability seems to be circumstantial and to fluctuate in a rhythmic way; our social hunger waxes and wanes as the tide. Of course, some people seem to spend a lot of time with others, seem to be chronic extroverts. But most are not, and even those who are seemingly gregarious all the time, may not be. To be sure about the degree of gregariousness we would have to watch them all the time, and that's impossible. Nonetheless, it may be useful for observers of human conduct to distinguish between the more gregarious and the less gregarious, or, as Jung, Myers, and a host of others say, the extroverts and the introverts. Once again, words are needed to assist us in forming an image of each type that is consistent with the more general words. The following sixteen words have been selected for their categorical accuracy and for their image value (Myers-Briggs terms are appended to indicate correlation, but not identity):

	IDEALISTS	RATIONALS	GUARDIANS	ARTISANS
RoleDirective	Mentors NFj	Organizers NTj	Monitors SJt	Operators SPt
Extroverted (e)	Pedagogue	FieldMarshal	Supervisor	Promoter
Introverted (i)	Prophet	Planner	Inspector	Crafter
RoleInformative	Advocates NFp	Engineers NTp	Conservators SJf	Players SPf
Extroverted (e)	Revealer	Inventor	Provider	Performer
Introverted (i)	Healer	Designer	Protector	Composer

The Eight Portraits of Character. The preceding portrayals are about the intellectual, motivational, emotional, and social traits of the eight personalities named in this book. The claim is that the two kinds of Artisans, that is, Operators and Players, are alike in most respects, but differ in many ways owing to their differences in directiveness in defining role relationships. So it is with the Guardians, Rationals, and Idealists. Since the difference in directiveness and informativeness is so detectable, even to casual inspection, it seemed useful to present eight, instead of four, portraits, at the cost of repetition of those traits common to both. If the portraits seem to redound upon one another, it is only because they do redound. On the other hand, since the difference between extroversion and introversion, that is, between degrees of gregariousness or sociability, is observable only if one follows the observed from time to time and from situation to situation, it is not useful to devise separate portraits for extroverts and introverts. In other words, there is very little difference that can be observed between the extroverted and introverted variants of the eight types because when two persons are interacting overtly, it is difficult to tell which of them is the more gregarious.

The Operators

Artisanship. The most important thing to understand about Operators[1] is that they are Artisans in their makeup and so are very similar to Players. But Operators operate on the environment, operate on anything and anybody. They are action oriented, like the other Artisans, but not just any kind of action will do; their orientation is to exercise their manipulative skills on the immediate concrete environment.

RoleDirectives. Operators are proactive in defining role relationships, which means that they will make the first move and stand ready to cope with any countermove, or exploit any compliance, that follows their initiative. In this they're tough minded—"When the going gets tough the tough get going." Not a bad motto for them. This trait is very noticeable in those Operators who are quite confident of their ability to gain the confidence of others. They'll do

---

[1] Operators are likely to score high on the S, P, and T scales of the Myers-Briggs Type Indicator and Temperament Sorter, the index of correlation probably in the neighborhood of sixty percent (.6).

or say whatever they have to to get their way. They are not out to please nearly as much as the other Artisans, the Players, but are competitive, seeking to outdo, overtake, outmaneuver, or best whomever they contest. Theirs is competitiveness, not showmanship, while the Players are given more to showmanship than competition. Operators would rather outsmart others than please them, not that they are averse to giving pleasure, but that being top dog is more important to them.

Concrete Pragmatism. Operators are concrete. They operate on the immediate concrete environment, and so are concrete in everything they do, just like the Players. They have no use for abstractions, considering them a boring waste of time and largely "BS", as they are likely to put it, useful to others perhaps but not them. A thing must be useful to interest the Operators, immediately useful, concretely useful, otherwise who needs it? In their insistence on things being useful the Operators have something in common with the Rationals; both are pragmatic, but in a different way. Operators are concretely pragmatic, while Rationals are abstractly pragmatic, the former utilitarian, the latter efficient. To the Operator it is use, and not efficiency, that matters, and that's all that matters. They are interested in what *actually* happens, never mind why, while the Rationals are focused on *why* and look upon what actually happens as mere data confirming or denying what they suppose to be true.

Social Impact. For Operators social impact is a necessity, even for those who appear to be aloof. One must be felt as a presence, even if only in resistance to the status quo. To be totally without influence, to make no difference at all in human affairs, is like being deprived of oxygen. Operators need to be potent, to affect the course of events. They see those who allow themselves to be pushed around as deserving of what they get. This doesn't mean Operators don't weaken, with aging or illness for example, but they try more than others to hang on to whatever social effectiveness they possess and avoid the onset of powerlessness as best they can.

Adventure. The Operators rarely miss a chance for adventure. If it means they must walk away from a good job they just might pay that price. It is they who say "make hay while the sun shines," "opportunity knocks but once," "who hesitates is lost," and the like. They do not hesitate. It is this notorious venturesomeness that no doubt prompted some psychologists to refer to the Artisans, Operators and Players alike, as the Sensation-Seeking Personality. Venturesomeness makes routine actions something to avoid. To have to do something because it's supposed to be done, or supposed to be done a certain way, challenges their waywardness. This is not to say they won't do what they're supposed to do, or do it in the prescribed way, or even do something over and over again. They may or may not, depending on how they feel at the moment. But they'll turn the activity into play if they can, and if they must repeat an action, they'll turn that into variations on a theme, such as, for instance, target practice. It is well to bear in mind the distinction between routine, something Operators and Players alike steer clear of, and perfecting a performance by repetition, something both will do inordinately because they act variably instead of repetitiously.

Hunting. As for the instincts attributed to humans, the Operators, like the Players, are more strongly inclined to hunting and less strongly inclined to territoriality and herding, while their inclination to medicine can even be weak and short lived, if it impells them at all. Also, many Operators tend to become attached to the tools they collect as time goes by, especially their vehicles and weapons.

Excitement. Operators are excitable. They are almost as excitable as Players. They enjoy getting hyped up and can tolerate a lot of excitement even for long periods without apparent bad effects, their operations even improving the more excited they are. However, just as they are quick to get excited, they are just as quick to get bored and, being on the tough side, they are not at all reluctant to let whoever is around them at the time know just how fed up they are with whatever dull routine they are supposed to follow. This excitability enables Operators to be oblivious to pain or fatigue, depending, of course, on what they're doing. If they're caught up in some chosen activity, grasped by the action itself as by a magnet, then they are inured. They climb the mountain "because it's there," not to get to the other side. Operation is for itself, not something else. The rest of us endure pain in our efforts, but the Operators are not making effort in our sense; they are operating rather, and so need not endure anything. Some say of Operators that during their continuing actions they are dedicated, but this is neither dedication, commitment, nor devotion. It is, rather, a kind of repetition entrancement, impelling the Operators to continue the action that has caught them in its web.

Boldness. Daring is a virtue to cultivate. Even more than their Player Artisan counterparts, the Operators require themselves to be macho. On the other hand the greatest of vices, and the one to feel the most guilty about, is what they call chickening out. Indeed, it is probably true that most Operators are somewhat bolder than the rest of us since they focus on their chances of success and remain oblivious to their chances of failure.

Skills Repertoire. Operators, like other Artisans, are proud of their skills. Should they perform awkwardly or

fashion something ugly, this can be a source of embarrassment, while lapses of responsibility or integrity or even ingenuity scarcely give them a twinge. No, their self-esteem
rests squarely and all but exclusively on their behavioral effectiveness and not on dependability or such abstract traits
as ingenuity and integrity, so trying to shame them for being
irresponsible or dishonest or lacking in ingenuity is, fortunately, futile.

Impulse. The Operator Artisans trust their impulses implicitly. What they mean by expressions like "strike while
the iron is hot" or "go for broke when you're on a roll" is
that their impulses can be trusted to lead them in the right
direction. Action born of impulse is more gratifying than
purposeful action, and if required to act for some end, the
end served is not allowed to influence execution. Action for
the Operator is an end in itself; it is self-directed, self-
leading, contains its own imperatives, the latter not to be
subordinated to mere regulations. Indeed, regulations inspire no faith whatsoever in the Operators. They figure that
rules are made up by those who can't do anything well in
order to curb those who can. Not only do they trust their
impulses, they act impulsively and without apology. For instance, they may take off just because "it seemed to be the
thing to do at the time." Popular films of the '60s and '70s,
like *Easy Rider, Cool Hand Luke, Five Easy Pieces* (and a raft
of Clint Eastwood westerns, e.g. *High Plains Drifter*) tended
to admire this impulsivity, even to glorify its tough, fugitive
way of life. The point is that the Operators don't intend or
plan to do something, whether constructive or destructive;
they simply do it when the impulse strikes them, oblivious
to both causes and consequences.

Virtuosity. Owing to their somewhat whimsical view of
others the Operators are not given to admiration very much,
but when they are, probably the only people they admire
are the prodigies, those rare individuals who in following

their impulses are perfect in their operations and are virtuosos of action. Just as they admire and envy the virtuoso, so they are scornful of the fumbling neophyte.

Awareness of Variation. The Operators' intellectual strength is in their consciousness of variations, an awareness of the minute thematic changes and alterations. Thus the Operators are very sensitive to the syntonic, symphonic, and confluent. For example, sights, sounds, and motions that harmonize and fit each other seem to come naturally and easily to Operators. But syntony is not the only kind of thematic changes the Operators are mindful of. Another long suit is a keen awareness of expedients, shortcuts, and quick fixes. They are on to anything and everything immediately useful. Nor does consciousness of variation preclude consciousness of convention. Rather, it presupposes it. Hence, Operators are also quite aware of the customary ways of doing things, of traditions, of standard operations. Not that they are prone to observe them, but they are not unaware of them. On the other hand, cognizance of change is not without penalty, in this case a kind of obliviousness to integration and synthesis. Focus on variation, alas, does not conduce to global, holistic, and diffuse awareness.

Optimistic Outlook. The Operators are the supreme optimists. The next shot will be a lucky one, never mind the fact that the last several have fizzled. The past is water under the bridge, so forget it! Operators *feel* lucky and perhaps that's why they seem to be cheerful. They *are* cheerful, in fact, because what comes next is bound to be a break, a windfall, something enjoyable.

Cynical Denial. But the Operators are also the supreme cynics, for they have no illusions about what others are up to. They know it is best to look a gift horse in the mouth; they know all too well that altruism can have hidden payoffs. They see our feet of clay and, forewarned, are invulnerable to disillusionment. They *expect* us to be self-serving and their expectations are usually met. It is true that Prometheus transformed us from clay to flesh and made us like the gods, but the Operators, cynics all, know all too well that we were, alas, left with feet of clay, *all too human.*

GoGetters. Operators, like their cousin Players, are go-getters. Given their keen perception of immediately useful concrete objects, including people, they are well equipped for such activity. Scrounging and foraging is even exciting to them because it is so active and because it puts to good use their natural intellectual ability. The movies *The Great Escape, Stalag 17,* and *King Rat,* each with remarkable accuracy, depict the incredible skill of the Operator scroungers as prisoners of war.

Mobility. For Operator Artisans the home is either a fraternity or sorority, insisting as they do that each member is equal to all other family members in mobility regardless of age, gender, or accomplishment. They neither understand nor accept a hierarchy in the family should this be imposed upon the members' activities by a parent, whether they themselves are parent or offspring. As children, the older they get the more open their defiance of those family rules of conduct that accord more freedom of movement to some than to others. And woe betide the Guardian type parent who tries to force teenage Operators to conform to any rules that confine their movements too stringently for their taste.

Conservator Spouse. As spouses the Operators are best off if they can find a Conservator type Guardian to give them anchorage and to welcome them home from their frequent excursions. Operators are most charming when they curry favor from others, and it is not at all difficult for them to charm the Conservator, the latter on the lookout for someone to conserve. This charm can be turned toward any other type of personality (and often is), but other types are not as forgiving of waywardness as the Conservator, so that marriages to other types may require more adjustments on the part of both partners, except that the Operator is unlikely to change his or her habits so that the changes must be made by the spouse. The Operators need the stability and patience of the Conservators to help them back home and in the fold, otherwise they may wander too long and too far into some frontier. Greely said "Go West young man!" Operators do.

Learning the Arts. The school harbors special problems for the Operators, problems shared only by the other Artisans. True, owing mainly to their harmonic and expedient imagination and perception they can both learn and teach the arts very well, indeed, far more easily than letters, sciences, or business. But unfortunately the school is not, and never has been, equipped with adequate personnel, materiel, or plans to teach a wide variety of arts other than sports. Most Operators are tough enough to avoid most of the assignments given them by most teachers at most levels for most subjects. The consequence is that they learn very little at school and drop out as early as they can, most of them while in the 9th grade. School is boring to many Operators, especially those who major in recess. Some of them, being more active than other children, do some things they have not been assigned to do, to the annoyance of the teacher. Some teachers get after these children, usually unsuccessfully, and in many cases the Operators, the older they get, will openly defy them. Despite a curriculum and instructional methods that offer them little, a few manage to stay in school long enough to get a teaching credential and so can be rather exciting teachers because their natural method of teaching is to *show* the learners *how* to do things. Even these, however, do not stay with teaching very long, since it's not very exciting to them.

The Failing School. The school's failure to educate the Operator and Player Artisans has resulted in a disastrous remedy. Naturally, if the Artisans don't do their school work their clerical skills do not improve and, because they're bored and restless, they move around much more than their classmates. The parents blame the school, as they should, but the school blames the child. He's "dyslexic," has "minimal brain disfunction," is "hyperactive," has a "learning disability." Therefore, says the school, he "needs medication." Then some well-meaning but ill-advised physician prescribes massive daily doses of some *stimulant* drug, parroting others' assumption that the stimulant has a "paradoxical effect" of acting as a depressant. The victim is thus given his daily fix and its false high, his teacher claiming that he's "calmer and works better." Who wouldn't be with that big a fix? And of course the child need not aspire to much; after all, what can you expect of a person with a bent brain? And later on? No, the child's real problem is the school, not his brain; his brain is just fine. Those who, despite the school's failure to be useful to them, manage to develop their inherent artisan talents are of enormous value to the society in that they fight our enemies, entertain us, and govern us. Too bad that most of these talents are nipped in the bud by early countereducative frostbite.

Tactical Work. At work the Operators are especially suited to devising tactics in action, which is to say maneuvering to overcome the immediate obstacles that block their actions. This is their strength, perfecting concrete actions and eliminating ineffective motions. Operators, like Players, are born artisans. This means that they have natural talent in the formation of objects and performances that require variable actions. If art is defined broadly as any thematic action that is continuously varied to advance and complete the chosen theme, and is not confined merely to painting, sculpture, dance, and music, then the Operators must be, along with the Players, conceded first place ahead of the other personalities. Take piloting as an example. Owing to their consciousness of minute change Operators are able to make those precise movements, which in flying or racing are mere pressures, that guide the vehicle precisely where it must go at precisely the right time. The story of Yeager illustrates this point. Sure, others can do the same thing, but not with the natural skill of the Operator. Artistic expression, as the fitting selection of free variables, is where the Operator shines. Those fortunate enough to have jobs that require their confluent and expedient variations are more fulfilled in their lives than those less fortunate. Despite their egalitarian and insubordinate nature the Operators can be leaders, even great ones. But they must be up front, sword in hand, leading the charge so to speak. They seize the moment and fully exploit whatever resources are at hand and capitalize on deficits and mistakes of their opponents. They are tactical leaders. Patton, Rommel, and countless other less well known battle leaders were cut from the same cloth. Their supreme sense of reality, timing, and expediency gives them the edge, and it's that edge that makes them winners. But their tactical leadership is not confined to battle, witness the spectacular tactical prowess of both Roosevelts.

Playing Games. At play the game is the Operators' choice of recreation, especially one they can participate in, though they aren't averse to watching all sorts of sporting events. They'll get into games of any kind, the more games the better. Expert poker and pool players, to cite two extreme examples, can play for days, without stopping, and don't seem to get tired doing it.

Festal Grouping. Some Operator Artisans get involved with community groupings, such as clubs and churches, in one way or another. When they do, their interest is usually not in the ceremonies and rituals of the group, or in the inspiration provided by the group, and they ignore any rational issues altogether. No, it is the festivities and frivolity that attract them and keep them in the fold, if they remain, and as often as not they are the ones who promote the festal events and the atmosphere of celebration.

Retaliation. Like all other personalities the Operator Artisans are sometimes forced by fear to turn to the negative side in their interpersonal relations. And like all other personalities, when troubled, they become tactical in denying any responsibility for their actions. The form of attack peculiar to the Operators is that of overriding or trampling on the values of others. Theirs is a game of retaliation in which they punish others by abusing them in some manner such as taking or injuring something valued. Their defensive tactics consist in acts of restitution in which they restore their lost verve by doing something exciting and getting even in the course of doing it. When their tactics become painfully noticeable they are sometimes called sadistic manics. Fortunately, in most cases such actions do not go on for long and the destruction is usually not irreversible.

Frequency. There are lots of Operators, maybe as many as eighteen percent, at least in the Caucasoid population, and since they, like their cousins, the Player Artisans, can be found wherever there is freely variable action, they are quite visible and therefore easy to identify. Most families have one such offspring, and, with increasing family size, even more. At school they are very much in evidence and very easy to identify owing to their liveliness. In the lower grades in ordinary classrooms there are about a half dozen such children in a class of thirty-two, but in the upper grades, especially the last two, most of these children have left school and refuse to return.

Promoters: The Gregarious Operators. When the Operators play their extroverted role they take up the task of promoting. Their totem deity is Pan, god of frivolity and chief satyr. Those Promoters with sufficient confidence in their ability to charm others into having confidence in them are without peer as entrepreneurs, diplomats, troubleshooters, and negotiators. They seem to be able to use others as foils to test their mettle, and in a sense they operate people much as the less gregarious Operators operate tools, and in that sense people are tools in their hands. Their approach to others has a theatrical flourish. They know just what to say to most everyone they meet, since they notice even minimal signals from others regarding their promotion. None are as socially sophisticated as they, none as suave and urbane. This charm enables them to be able diplomats and negotiators. They can operate smoothly and keep their cool in crises, since they do not stand around on ceremony and are quite aware of all expedients that can be put to immediate use. For instance, in negotiating on behalf of some organization, as far as they are concerned everything is negotiable, so they've got an edge on their opponents should the latter consider some asset or procedure as sacred and therefore not negotiable.

Crafters: The Seclusive Operators. When the Operators play their introverted role they can achieve mastery over those instruments with variable controls that extend and amplify human capabilities. Their totem deity is Ares, god of conquest, after whom they seem to model themselves. We are prudent to pay special attention to the mechanical talent the less gregarious Operators seem to be born with. It can show up early in childhood if we but allow it. A tool is any mechanical device that extends our powers; a variable tool varies our powers. The vehicle, musical instrument, cutting device, and weapon are but four examples of the plethora of variable tools that surrounds us. The Crafters can be incomparable surgeons; they can also be incomparable pilots of all manner of vehicles, incomparable musicians, and incomparable warriors. Consider the latter. A born hunter, the Crafter finds one tool that can be especially attractive to him or her: the weapon. The Crafter

Operators can wield the weapon with lethal virtuosity. They even look upon the duel form of combat as an art form. Foss, Boyington, Bong, Fonck, von Richtoffen, Bishop, Rickenbacker—all were artistic duelists in the operation of the winged machine gun.

The Players

Artisanship. Players[1] are Artisans and so are in many ways just like the Operators. However, they are different from Operators in many ways. Especially they are more playful than Operators, indeed the most playful of all the types. This playfulness is so apparent in their conduct that it is useful to call them 'the players'.

Cooperative Informatives. Players are informative in letting others know of their willingness, or resistance, to play the roles assigned to them. This means that they will rarely make the first move in defining the roles they are willing to play, and they stand ready to respond, favorably if they can, to the moves of roledirectors. On those occasions when they do initiate definitions of role relationships they do so with some discomfort and some apology. They like to respond to others favorably and are prone to do real favors

---

[1] Players are likely to score high on the S, P, and F scales of the Myers-Briggs Type Indicator and Temperament Sorter, the index of correlation probably in the neighborhood of sixty percent (.6).

for others in ways that will give others immediate pleasure.
They are sensuous, able to titillate others', and their own,
senses by offerings of music, dance, food and drink, and
other sorts of amusement. Nor can they be said to be competitive like the Operators even though they love to play
first fiddle. Theirs is showmanship, not competitiveness.
They would excite and please, not overtake and outdo. Players hunger to star in whatever is shown in their chosen
medium, love to put on a show.

Concrete Pragmatism.
Players are concrete, every bit
as concrete as Operators. They have little interest in and no
patience with abstractions, considering them a boring waste
of time. Abstractions, symbols, and analogies are so much
''BS'', some of them will say, useful to some perhaps, but
not to them. Things must be useful to interest the Players,
immediately useful, concretely useful, otherwise ignore
them and find something that is. In a way the Players are
like the abstract pragmatists, the Rationals, but only in that
they are pragmatic. In contrast, they are utilitarian pragmatists, not efficiency pragmatists. It is use, and not efficiency, that matters, and that's all that matters. What means
something to the Players is *what* actually happens, never
mind why, while the Rationals are focused on *why* and look
upon what in fact happens as mere data confirming or denying what they suppose to be true.

Impelling Actions.
Players are like Operators in their
ability to ignore pain or fatigue. It, of course, depends on
what they're doing. If they're caught up in the traction of
some chosen composition or performance, grasped as by a
magnet by the action itself, then they don't notice either
pain or fatigue. They climb the mountain ''because it's
there,'' not to get to the other side. Play is for itself, not
something else. We may endure and bear pain in our
traverse, but the Players are not traversing, just playing, and
so need not bear up under or outlast anything. Those of

differing nature say of Players that during their continuing actions they are dedicated to the sport or show or whatever. But this is not dedication. It is rather like being in a trance. The tractor beam so to speak gets them to continue their performance quite without their having to exert their will.

Hedonism. Players are hedonic. A life without some pleasure is not worth living. All other motives are subordinated to pleasure and expressed in its service. Even more, they are Epicurean, in that they view the joyless life as somewhat immoral. They want to have fun. Life is a game to be played and is not for keeps. If it's not fun, do something else whenever possible! Does this mean that Players won't do things that aren't fun? Yes and no. They'll do them if they have to, but they're itching to get to the fun part or to go elsewhere where more fun is possible.

Social Influence. Though they want pleasures, they *must have* impact on others, must be able to influence others in some way, make some sort of impression. This hunger for impact is what fuels their showmanship. The longing to perform is in some sense like oxygen-hunger. Deficits in impactfulness but increase their hankering for it.

Adventuresomeness. Though they want pleasures and need to be influencial, they actively seek adventures. They will latch onto any ventures that come their way. They are not averse to risk themselves just for the thrill of it. The adventurer must be free to take a chance when the opportunity to do so arises, so it is no surprise that the Players, like the Operator Artisans, are careful to avoid routine whenever possible. Their adventure-lust makes routine anathema to them, most of them regarding it as something to detour. This is not to say they won't do what they're supposed to do. They will , but with a twist so to speak. They are venturesome even with routines, much to the dismay of their supervisors. The distinction between routine performance and variations on a theme is important in understanding why the Artisans, Player and Operator alike, skate around the standard operating procedures prescribed by others. And it may be that this ever present venturesomeness of the Artisans is what prompted some psychologists to call them, along with the Operators, the Sensation-Seeking Personality.

Hunting Instinct. Players are in some sense like the rest of us, that is, endowed with those instincts attributed to humans. But the Players seem more strongly inclined to the hunting instinct and less strongly inclined to magic, herding, and medicine. Some have noted that the latter, nesting for a length of time, may be the weakest of the social imperatives in the case of Players.

Excitability. Players are excitable. Clearly the most excitable of all the types. And excitement seems to add to their enjoyment. They, like other Artisans, can tolerate high levels of excitement for long periods of time, apparently without cost to them. It is when they're excited that they're at their performing best. But this easy excitability has a price tag, namely that they are also quickly bored after doing too much too fast. Alternation between hyperactivity and ennui is one of the hallmarks of the Players, almost as noticeable as their playfulness.

Expertise. The self-esteem of Players comes from how well they do, either in creating things or in performing. Clumsy performance or poor workmanship can embarrass them more than anything else. For instance, lapses of inventiveness, honesty, or accountability hardly even bother them, especially the latter. Their self-regard is based mainly on their performance repertoire and not on those things that make others feel good about themselves.

Boldness. Players look upon daring as a virtue worth cultivating and being chicken a vice to feel guilty about. And they usually are rather bold, not so much because they master their fears, rather because their carefree nature inclines them to concentrate more on what they are doing and less on possible dangers.

Impulsivity. Players are not only impulsive, they have great faith in their impulses. What they mean by expressions like "strike while the iron is hot" or "go for broke when you're on a roll" is that their impulses can be trusted to lead them in the right direction. In stark contrast, Players, like Operators, have no faith whatsoever in rules and regulations. They figure that rules are made up by those who can't do anything well to curb those who can. In all probability the only people they admire are the prodigals of action, those rare individuals who in following their impulses are perfect in their products and performances. Just as they admire and envy the virtuoso, so they are scornful of the fumbling amateur.

Consciousness of Variation. The Players intelligence lies in their consciousness of variations, an acute awareness of even minute variations on a theme, a sensitivity to syntonic, symphonic, and confluent changes. Sights, sounds, and motions that harmonize and fit each other seem to come naturally to Players. But this is not the only kind of thematic change they are sensitive to. They can also be quite cognizant of expedients, of shortcuts, and of quick fixes. Anything immediately useful cannot escape them. The Players are especially attuned to color, line, texture, and shading, to touching, tasting, smelling, seeing, hearing, and moving, all in harmony. Rembrandt could see a single pixel of discordant color, Toscanini could hear one false note among thousands, Hemingway's words tasted and smelled and felt the waves. This kind of awareness presupposes rather than precludes awareness of convention. Thus, Operators are also quite aware of the customary, traditional, and standard ways of doing things, even though they are not prone to observe them. It is more a need to know what to change. On the other hand cognizance of change is not without penalty, in this case a kind of obliviousness to integration and synthesis. Focus on variation, alas, does not conduce to global, holistic, and diffuse awareness.

Optimistic Outlook.

The Player is the supreme optimist. The next shot will be a lucky one, never mind the fact that the last several have fizzled. The past is water under the bridge so forget it! Players *feel* lucky, and perhaps that's why they appear to the observer as chipper and cheerful. They *are* cheerful, cheerful because what comes next is bound to be a break, a windfall, something enjoyable. Perhaps it is this perspective that makes the Players kind and generous beyond measure. And their kindness is unconditional. They are especially sensitive to the pain and suffering of others, particularly small children and animals. Perhaps it is their kind and generous nature that makes them attractive to children and animals alike. Of course other types can be kind and generous, but this trait seems to be woven into the warp and woof of the Player's makeup.

Cynical Denial.

But here also is the supreme cynic. Players have no illusions about what others are up to. They know better than most that it is best to look a gift horse in the mouth. They know all too well that those of us who offer altruism omit mention of what we get out of it. Seeing with full clarity our feet of clay the Players are invulnerable to disillusionment. They *expect* us to be self-serving and their expectations are usually met.

GoGetters.

Players, like their cousin Operators, are gogetters. Given their keen perception of immediately useful concrete objects, including people, they are well equipped for such activity. Scrounging and foraging is even exciting to them because it is so active and because it puts to good use their natural intellectual abilities.

Mobility. For Players the home is either a fraternity or sorority, insisting as they do that each member is equally free to do as he or she pleases, regardless of age, gender, or accomplishment. They neither understand nor accept the family hierarchy should one be imposed upon the family by a parent, even if they are themselves parents. They insist on being free to do what they please, how they please, when they please. They see no reason why those older than they should be any more freewheeling than they. The older they get the more open their defiance of those family rules that accord greater freedom to some than to others.

Monitor Spouse. As spouses the Players are best off if they can find an Monitor Guardian type to give them anchorage and to check them over when they come home from their frequent excursions. Players are most charming when they curry favor from others, and it is not at all difficult for them to charm the Monitor, the latter on the lookout for someone to supervise and inspect. This charm can be turned toward any other type of personality (and often is), but other types are surprised by the waywardness of the Players while the Monitor is not. Indeed it is this frivolity that attracts the Monitor to the Player in the first place, so it doesn't catch him or her off balance when it shows up. The Players need the stability and patience of the Monitors to help them back into the fold, otherwise they may wander too long and too far into some frontier. They, like the Operators, are inclined to take Greely's advisory to "Go West."

Learning the Arts. The school has special problems awaiting the Players when they come to attend. True, owing mainly to their syntonic and expedient observation and imagination they can both learn and teach the arts very well, indeed, far more easily than letters, sciences, or business. But few schools are equipped with personnel, materiel, or instructional models that are necessary to equip the Players with an artisan repertoire. The school abjectly fails to meet the needs of the Artisans, especially the Players. Most Players somehow manage to avoid most of the assignments given them by most teachers at most levels for most subjects. So what they do learn at school cannot be attributed to the instructional program. The fare is so unsavory and profitless that they drop out as early as they can, most of them while in the 9th grade. They're bored. Recess, music, and sports may interest some of them, for a while. Some of them, being more active than other children, develop skills for annoying the teachers, and the teachers struggle with them as best they can, but with little success. Despite a curriculum and instructional methods that offer them little, a few manage to get a teaching credential and even become exciting teachers (for Artisans like themselves), because their natural method of teaching is to *show* the learners *how* to do things. Even these, however, do not stay with teaching very long, since it's not very exciting to them.

The Failing School. The school's failure to educate the Artisans has resulted in a disastrous remedy. Naturally, if the Artisans, Operators as well as Players, don't do their school work, their clerical skills do not improve and, because they're bored and restless, they move around much more than their classmates. The parents justifiably blame the school, but the school blames the child. He's "dyslexic," they say, has "minimal brain disfunction," is "hyperactive," has a "learning disability." Therefore, they say, he needs "medication." So some well-meaning but ill-advised physician prescribes massive daily doses of some *stimulant* drug. Given his daily fix and its false high, his teacher claims he's "calmer and works better." Who wouldn't be with that big a fix? And of course the child need not aspire to much; after all, what can you expect of a person with a bent brain? And later on? No, the child's real problem is the school, not his brain; his brain is just fine. Those Players who, despite the school's failure, manage to develop their inherent artisan talents are of enormous value to the society in that they fight our enemies and entertain us. Too bad that most of these talents are nipped in the bud by early miseducative frostbite.

Tactical Work. On the job the Players are especially suited to tactical maneuvers. They perfect their mode of operation and eliminate ineffective motions. They have natural talent in creating things and behavior patterns that require variation on their part. Broadly defined, art is any thematic action continuously varied to advance and complete a given theme. Art should not be thought of as limited to only painting, sculpture, and music. It is much more, such as to include all variable controls of tools. So defined, it must be conceded that the Players and Operators are peerless in such artful actions. Consider the example of painting, sculpting, or dancing. Owing to their consciousness of variation Players are able to select just that option of coloring, cutting, or moving that fits the total form of the work they are producing. Art, as selection of free variables, is the arena where the Players shine. Fortunate indeed are those who get jobs that exercise their syntonic and expedient variations, and most unfortunate are those Artisans who never get the chance at such exercise.

Playing Games. Players seem to play a lot; the game is their choice of recreation, especially one they can participate in and not just watch. Games of any kind, the more games the better. Poker and pool players, to cite two extreme examples, can play for days, without stopping, and don't seem to get tired doing it.

Festal Grouping. Some Player Artisans get involved with clubs, churches, and meetings of one kind or another. When they do their interest is usually not with the ceremonies and rituals, or with the inspirational talks or conversations, and they simply ignore theoretical and definitional issues. It is rather the festivities that attract them and keep them in the group, and as often as not they are the ones that promote the frivolity and the atmosphere of celebration.

Retaliation. Like all other personalities the Player Artisans are sometimes forced by fear to turn to the negative side and do things unconsciously and involuntarily, things that bother others and seem to have no payoff. And like all other personalities they deny any responsibility for such actions, but they do so in their own unique way. They blame others for what they do, and so they start up games of retaliation in which they punish others by acts of self-abuse. These games may be seen as defensive tactics, acts of restitution in which they restore the excitement they regard as rightfully theirs at the same time they get even. When their tactics become obtrusive the professionals are inclined to call them masochistic manics. Fortunately, in most cases such actions do not go on for long and the destruction is not always irreversible.

High Frequency. There are lots of Players, eighteen percent or so, at least in the Caucasoid population, and since they, along with their cousins, the Operators, can be found wherever there is freely variable action, they are quite visible and therefore easy to identify. Most families have one such offspring, and, with increasing family size, even more. At school they are very much in evidence and very easy to identify owing to their liveliness. In the lower grades in ordinary classrooms there are about a half dozen such children in a class of thirty-two, but in the upper grades, especially the last two, most of these children have left school and don't come back.

Performers: The Gregarious Players. When feeling gregarious the Players take up the task of putting on a show to entertain others. Their totem deity is Eros, god of love, after whom many of them seem to fashion their performances. Their social interest lies in stimulating others, in arousing pleasant emotions in others, in evoking enjoyment. In a sense they may be thought of as seductive, able as they are to distract others from their overly serious concerns and titillate their senses. They radiate warmth and optimism, are smooth, witty, voluble, charming. They avoid being alone for very long, and have no difficulty finding company, for they raise others' spirits with their contagious laughter and happy faces. They can banter continuously and are quite amusing to those in a recreational mood. Up on the latest fashions and fads of dress, food, drink, and entertainment, the gregarious Performer must be seen as the most entertaining of all the types. Intent on pleasing everybody as they are, they are sometimes seen as fickle. They give their love freely and seem not to expect anything in return.

Composers: The Seclusive Players. When feeling seclusive the Players take up the task of constituting aesthetic forms. Their totem deity is Aphrodite, god of beauty, after whom they seem to fashion themselves. These seclusive Players are not very sure of their social impact, seeming to be without social interest. But this is deceiving, for their social interest is just as strong as in those who put on a show for others without hesitation. They wish to favor others just as much as the Performers do, but with their compositions. They will perform, but only to display whatever they have composed, and such performance must be preceded by much rehearsal in private. The most obvious example is the songwriter who sings only his or her own songs. But we should not make the mistake of defining composition too narrowly, as, for instance, confined solely to music, painting, sculpture, and dance. Hundreds of other things are composed: films and shows, tapestry and pottery, sports and gags, to name only a few. Jack Benny was a superb gagman as well as a superb performer of his own gags; gagmen become comedians just as piano and violin players become orchestrators. The Composers who are truly private people seem to have little interest in developing their speech and writing, preferring rather to keep their fingers on the pulse of life rather than just talk about it. This close attunement to reality can, in some, occasion a kind of breach with language so that without much practice in verbal communications the inarticulateness of youth remains. Speech, for the Composers, is not the best way to express oneself; artful composition is.

The Monitors

Guardianship. Monitors[1] practice guardianship just as diligently as Conservators, but in a strikingly different way. Conservators protect and nurture their charges, while Monitors inspect and supervise them. All Guardians stand as safeguards against the depredations of nature and man. They insure us against loss, defeat, disappointment, setbacks, and disasters on the one hand, and deviations, violations, delinquencies, and unauthorized actions on the other. They would prevent these untoward events if they could; failing this, then they would undo the harm done as best they can. They are the willing and natural fiduciaries and trustees, those we trust to keep us safe from harm, both from being victims and from victimizing others.

Cooperative Directives. Monitors are cooperative. They cooperate with superiors religiously and carry out

---

[1] Monitors are likely to score high on the S, J, and T scales of the Myers-Briggs Type Indicator and Temperament Sorter, the index of correlation probably in the neighborhood of sixty percent (.6).

orders without fail and to the letter. Moreover, when they
have subordinates or dependents they expect them to do ex-
actly as they, the Monitors, do in relation to *their* superiors:
proceed with unquestioning obedience. Rank, they are
prone to say, has its obligations, but it also has its privileges.
Monitors are proactive in defining the roles they and others
are to play. They do not hesitate to indicate what others are
supposed to do or not do. Nor are they uncomfortable in
issuing role directives. Telling others what to do is a matter of duty, so they are not at all reluctant to determine these
reciprocal relations between themselves and others. De-
mands, commands, requests, and questions come easily to
the tongue and are not disqualified as mere information. In
this respect they are quite unlike the other Guardians, the
Conservators, who issue roledirectives with more than a little discomfort and unease.

Concrete Expressions. Monitors are concrete. Analogies
and abstractions are impractical, having little to do with
reality. The table of particulars and standard operating
procedures are what count. Monitors mean business on this
matter and are prepared to take the responsibility to be
tough on those in their charge who deviate from the particular and the standard, or are in danger of doing so. Their
toughness has to do with productive and ceremonial conduct, not play, and not imagination. If people wish to play
or daydream, fine, as long as they do it on their own time.
But the dreaming or playful member, whether employee,
subordinate, offspring, or for that matter, spouse, should not
be surprised when reprimanded for wasting time while on
duty. The top sergeant will not put up with such nonsense.

Economics. The primary drive of the Guardians, both
Monitors and Conservators, is economic. Although ethics is
important, it does not compare with economics, while
merely aesthetic and theoretical issues take a back seat
until and unless the problem of economics has been solved.

And for most Guardians, Monitors and Conservators alike, the economic problem is never solved such as to remain the first priority throughout life. This means they hold themselves and others accountable to be industrious always, even as children and after retirement.

Security. Monitors and Conservators alike are in an eternal search for security. The search goes on such that regardless of the amount of acquisition and insurance, the storage bin seems for them all but empty. This trait has inclined some behavioral scientists to name the Guardians, both Monitor and Conservator, the Security Seeking Personality.

Membership. Groups attract them like magnets, perhaps because membership fulfills in some degree their search for security. They need to belong just as they need food, water, and air. They hunger for membership and must have it at all times. And so the event, or its anticipation, of being cast out or banished from the fold is most aversive to them. Added to this, or perhaps underlying it, of the supposed instincts of mankind, herding has a stronger pull for the Monitor than all others. They the herders and others the herdees, their very instincts in the service of their need of membership. Also there seems to be some attraction in hunting and in medicine, but magic is a mere vestige. And ownership, like membership, is of vital import to Monitors; they can even cherish what belongs to them, especially if the possession has been owned for a long period by them and theirs. On the other hand they reject poverty with all the force they can muster, striving all their lives to ward it off.

Concern. Monitors are very serious, especially about procedures. They tend to worry a lot and let others know they're worried. Their main concern is about what sorts of delinquencies, chicanery, misdemeanors, and derelictions of duty are impending. These are serious matters to them even when occurrence is unlikely. They can get into a snit over this, and may stew and pother about it to anyone in earshot. But they do not rest their case with mere apprehension, for their worries can be supplanted by gloomy evaluations of the bad things that have already happened. Yet they are not at all clear about what reverses make them feel so bad. Even so, to try to reassure them for their worries, or to jolly them up for their despondency, is fruitless. Happily, either mood is time limited and will pass without any changes in the real world.

Responsibility. Monitors feel proud of their accountability and of their strength in holding others accountable. They hold that they can be trusted with large estates, the larger the estate, the greater their self-esteem on being so trustworthy. If nothing else, they say, "You can count on us to fulfill our obligations and honor our contracts." Here lies the source of their self-esteem. But here also lies a ready source of shame, for dereliction of duty is a greater source of chagrin and embarrassment than, for instance, dishonesty, inability, or stupidity. No greater wound to pride can be given than to attribute irresponsibility to them. The Monitors hide from others' sight when, for whatever reason, they fail to be accountable.

Beneficence. As for feeling good about themselves, with all their seeming miserliness, still the Monitors consider generosity the greatest of all virtues and greed the greatest of the vices. Should they be penurious or stingy, which they well may be in the service of securing estate, they may suffer some pangs of guilt as payment. They, like their cousin Conservators, tend to feel indebted always however much they have discharged their debts.

Authority. The Monitors, more than any type other than Conservators, can put their trust in authority, while they seem unable to trust those who are licentious and take the law into their own hands. Those without proper credentials cannot be counted on, and it is fitting and proper that government agencies see to it that licenses and permits are given only to those passing the scrutiny of those officially sanctioned to issue such authorizations.

Aristocrats. The admiration of the Monitors goes unwittingly and spontaneously to aristocrats, plutocrats, and persons of high status. Just as unwittingly and involuntarily they cannot help being scornful of barbarians and the unacculturated.

Orthodox Awareness. The Monitors are probably more orthodox and convention conscious, more observant of custom and tradition, than all other types, save their fellow Guardians, the Conservators. They seek to establish standard operating procedures whenever possible. All things and all actions must conform to the standards set forth by the group. Opinions approved by established groups are the only ones to hold firmly. Hypotheses must be subjected to the scrutiny of authorities, changes to the tribunals of institutions, rebellion and deviation from the norm summarily punished. The Monitors' intelligence is mainly associative, which is to say they can imagine or observe, as the case may be, conventional juxtapositions and connections. Their thought, in other words, is essentially linear, additive, and correlational, such that, for instance, arithmetic and spelling come more easily to them than, say, the geometries and algebras. Likewise they are very sensitive to the quantitative. That is, they can be extraordinarily effective in imagining or observing matters of degree. But their conventional consciousness does not make them unaware of change. Indeed they can be very sensitive to change, if only to prevent it. Given, as they are, to constancy far more than to differentiation, to standardization far more than analysis, it is sometimes hard for them to focus on the latter. For that matter, they are more cognizant of implications than they are of differences and distinctions.

Fatalistic Outlook.
As with other kinds of temperament, the Monitors have both positive and negative ways of regarding their surroundings. Monitors, like Conservators, are fatalists. Things are what they are because they were fated to be that way. Events are inevitable, the course of our lives set, either by the will of God or the inexorable rules of Mother Nature.

Pessimistic Denial.
But Monitors are pessimists too: Murphy was prophetic in saying "Everything that can go wrong, will"; Chicken Little was prudent in warning that "the sky is falling!"; and Aesop's Ant was circumspect in counseling grasshopper to "join me, and we shall together harvest in all haste, for cold winter lurks at fall's edge."

SafeKeeping.
Monitors and Conservators are scripted to act out a life of safekeeping, even as children and after retirement. This scenario shows up at home, at school, at work, at play, and at community meetings.

Hierarchy.
In the home they, even more than their cousin Conservators, insist that each member has a fixed place in a family hierarchy. Individualism and freedom of action are out and will not be tolerated. Elders are due both privileges and respect solely in virtue of their status. Even the older siblings have higher status than the younger. Members have certain duties they are to do. But it is not enough just to do them, they are to *want* to do their duty and for the *right* reason. Acting dutifully for the wrong reasons is not acceptable. Monitors are especially watchful over their offspring, some are even over-watchful, keeping them under their thumbs perhaps too long. The older their children the more

they supervise their activities and inspect their productions, together with appropriate admonitions and caveats regarding any deviations from seemly conduct. As offspring the Monitors are dependable and dutiful almost from infancy, and they usually respect their parents whether or not such respect is deserved. If, for example, they are punished by a parent, they do not hold it against that parent, and are likely, in retrospect at least, to say they deserved it.

Artisan Mates. Although they can safely marry many of the types, their best bet seems to be the Artisans, especially the Player Artisans. They seem able to put up with the frolics of the Players, though they may reprove them now and then and even punish them. But such reproof and punishment is like water off a duck's back when the recipient is a Player Artisan. Not so if the recipient is an Operator. In the latter case the Monitor soon learns to withhold most reproof and all punishment. Perhaps because the Monitors are rather straightlaced they find something attractive in the playfulness of the Player personality, especially in the latter's ability to bring cheer and recreation to the otherwise sober and downcast Monitors.

Learning Business. At school the Monitors, like other Guardians, teach and learn business activities and information better than the subject matter in letters, arts, or sciences. Their standardizing consciousness, associative and quantitative thought and perception give them the edge over others in the business field, for most operations in the world of goods and services require this sort of intellect. School, especially the first twelve grades, seems to have been made for the Guardians, especially the Monitors. They wish to do what they are supposed to above all else and rarely question the teacher's assignments, method of instruction, intentions, or authority. They are usually model students, conscientiously following each and every directive, doing all homework, doing it thoroughly, doing it on time. School was made for them and by them and, despite brief excursions to suit the Idealists, continues to serve them.

Materiel Work. At work, owing again to their associative and quantitative intellectual talents, Monitor Guardians, like Conservators, do best at storage, recording, measurement, retrieval, and dispatching of materiel. In this field they are incomparable, for no other arena of work is so well suited to standard operations and orthodox procedures. Clerical work can be very satisfying to them, the brighter ones becoming executives, office managers, accountants, bankers, brokers, underwriters, realtors, and the like.

Indulgent Recreation. At play, insofar as the Monitors take time to play—many never learn how—being catered to and indulged is recreational. While the Artisans are playing games with vigor and abandon, while the Idealists are lost in make-believe, and while the Rationals are carefully perfecting their skills, the Monitors are restfully taking surcease from their obligations as they are passively wined, dined, and entertained. To not have to be responsible for a little while is the best kind of play for these nose-to-the-grindstone people.

Ceremonial Grouping. High percentages of the Monitors join groups and attend meetings, and tend to be the mainstays of such groupings, whether club, church, PTA, or whatever. They meet with others for the rituals and ceremonies. Rationale, inspiration, and even festivities are OK, but these cannot substitute for the proper ceremonies. These must be observed to ensure continuity, stability, and to perpetuate the institution. That is to say, the rituals and ceremonies of their chosen groups are not negotiable, while rationale, inspiration, and festivity might be.

Frequency. The Monitors are necessary for keeping the lid on society and preventing chaos. It is fortunate that they abound in order to fulfill this ubiquitous task. It may be that there are as many as twenty percent in the Caucasian population, and since these people overtly foster the maintenance of groups, they are the most visible of all the personality types and the easiest to identify. Almost half of the families probably have at least one such parent, and with increasing family size, more than one Monitor offspring. There are lots of them in ordinary classrooms, comforting and even delighting the teachers (with their moral support), with perhaps eight in a class of thirty-two in the lower grades, while in the upper grades their percentage is much higher, given that Artisans steer clear of secondary schools.

Depression. When forced by fear to behave tactically toward others the Monitors, like other Guardian natures, deny their own responsibility by accusing others of abandoning them. Added to this they play the game of complaining of great burdens and losses that they must bear that have immobilized them, and so they imply that they ought to be exempt from ordinary obligations. Especially they can complain of fears for their health and concern for this or that body organ. Also they can complain of feelings of exhaustion. When such tactics become painfully noticeable to family and friends the Monitors are sometimes called the Neurasthenic or Hypochondriac Depressives. But such episodes are usually short lived and tend to give way to an upswing of feeling without interference from others or situational changes.

Supervisors: The Gregarious Monitors. When they feel gregarious Monitors take up the task of supervising the work and play of any and all of their charges. The totem deity of the extroverted Monitor is Themis, god of laws. Supervision means watching people working or playing or engaging in ceremonies. It means watching with one eye on behavior and the other on traditions and regulations. The person appointed supervisor is responsible to see to it that people behave in accord with agreed upon standards of conduct or face the agreed upon consequences for not doing so. Those Monitors who are comfortable playing their public roles most of the time, that is to say, gregarious or extroverted Monitors, gravitate to the supervisor role and, because they're so good at this job, stay with it. They'll read the riot act to anyone who steps out of line; they do this because they feel obligated to do it, and they're sometimes surprised the culprit is not grateful for such admonishment. We can depend on them to do their duty no matter how distasteful it may be. When the umpire throws a ballplayer out of the ballpark for abusive language he keeps the lid on the game, and that's what he's paid to do, keep order. Without the 'ump' there'd be no game. We don't like being called on the carpet for our goofs, but we are comforted as we see the other guy called to accounts.

Inspectors: **The Seclusive Monitors.** When they feel seclusive Monitors take up the task of inspecting the productions of any and all of their charges. The totem deity of the introverted Monitor is Demeter, god of the harvest. Inspection is taking a close look at something done, such as inspecting a crop ready for harvest, or careful scrutiny of a company's books. Such reviews are not cursory. Whatever is inspected is put under a magnifying glass so that no discrepancy or omission is overlooked. The inspectional Monitor doesn't miss anything, so keen is his or her perusal. And this is a matter of duty, an obligation to those who appointed him or her to the task. Those who are more comfortable in their private roles, those more seclusive or introverted, move inevitably, or should, to these inspectional tasks and, content with such activities, stay with them. Like their gregarious counterparts, the Supervisors, they are looking for deviation from standards, but unlike the Supervisors, they do not see it as their task to confront the deviator. It is enough, and certainly more comfortable, to report this to the authority who ordered the inspection. Of course we are not all too happy having our work gone over with a fine-toothed comb; but, alas, this phase of work is all too necessary. We can count on the inspectional Monitor to be thorough and painstaking to catch anything not up to snuff. We may not be grateful to the inspector who examines what we produce, but we are to the one who inspects the produce we buy.

The Conservators

Guardianship. The Conservator[1] is just as much a guardian as the Monitor, but in a strikingly different way. Conservators protect and nurture, while Monitors inspect and supervise. All Guardians, whether conserving or monitoring, stand as safeguards against the vicissitudes of life. The Conservators especially try to insure us against loss, defeat, disappointment, setbacks, calamities, catastrophies, and disasters. They want to prevent these bad things from happening if they can, but if they can't, they try to undo the harm as best they can. They are willing and able to serve as fiduciaries and trustees, and this role comes naturally to them. They enculturate and institutionalize in the interest of prevention.

Cooperative Informatives. Like other Guardians, they are cooperative in every way they can think of. But they differ from the other Guardians, the Monitors, in how they

---

[1] Conservators are likely to score high on the S, J, and F scales of the Myers-Briggs Type Indicator and Temperament Sorter, the index of correlation probably in the neighborhood of sixty percent (.6).

go about defining roles. They do not initiate role definitions. Or if they do, it is hesitantly and with some discomfort. They are content to let others suggest what roles they are to play, which suggestions they confirm or deny by informing the rolecaster of their willingness or unwillingness to be so cast. They give information about their social relations frequently and easily, directives, infrequently and uneasily. Their cooperation is carried out with almost religious fervor; orders are most often obeyed promptly and accurately. When they themselves have subordinates or dependents, they ask to be regarded and treated by them the same way the Conservators regard and treat *their* superiors—with gratitude, respect, and compliance. Unlike the Monitors, however, should they not get the gratitude, respect, and compliance due them, they usually bear this ignominy in silence, and are reluctant to confront such attitudes. They are very nice people, unfortunately at the price of stewing in their own juices in the face of ignominies.

Expressive Concreteness. Conservators are concrete in their expressions, every bit as down to earth as the other Guardians. They rarely traffic in analogies, symbolisms, and abstractions. Though they are tolerant of those who do, they consider such messages as rather impractical, having little to do with the real world. The inventory of supplies and the schedule of protective measures are what count. Conservators aren't kidding around on this matter and are prepared as an obligation to the group to favor those whom they serve with the utmost care in provender and security. Their favoring nature bids them to see to it that the real and present physical needs of those in their circle are met. Their messages, and the messages they listen to avidly, concern mainly concrete realities. Their excursions to the fifth plain of irreality are infrequent and short lived.

Economics. The primary drive of the Guardians, including Monitors and Conservators, is economic. They attempt

to solve the economic problem with a will, such that we
may think of them as having an economic will. Aesthetic,
ethical, and theoretical issues take a back seat until and unless the problems of economics have been satisfactorily dealt
with. And for most of them the economic problem is never
completely solved, so it remains first throughout life. They
hold themselves responsible to be industrious in every way
and at all times. This can be seen in their conduct even
when they are small children and after they have retired.
From this project they cannot retire because it is in their
nature to keep at it all their lives.

Security. Perhaps underlying an economic will is the Conservators' eternal search for security. The search goes on,
apparently an unreachable goal, such that regardless of the
amount of acquisition and insurance, in their view the
storage bin is half empty, the loaf of bread, half gone. This
trait has inclined some behavioral scientists to name both
the Conservator and Monitor Guardians, the Security Seeking Personality.

Membership. The Conservators seem to find some security in group membership, however, needing to belong as
they need food, water, and air. They hunger for belonging.
They must have it at all times. It is not negotiable, will not
be yielded up. And so the prospect of being cast out,
banished, or abandoned is anticipated with dread. Added to
this, of the supposed instincts of mankind, herding seems
to have a stronger pull for the Conservators than all others,
their very instincts put in the service of their need of membership. Medicine may have a strong imperative for them
also, while it is doubtful whether hunting or magic impels
them at all.

Proprietorship. Ownership, like membership, is of vital
import to Conservators, perhaps as important as it is for Monitors. They prize family possessions, the longer possessed,

the more cherished. Poverty, of course, is warded off with all the energy and effort required.

Seriousness. Conservators are concerned, very concerned. For them there is much to be concerned about. Society is decaying, morals and manners no longer as they were when their elders were young. There is much cause to worry and those who don't worry are seen as irresponsible. This over-concern about impending loss, injury, destruction, or defeat can be pervasive, even when such setbacks are highly unlikely. But this is not all, for the concerns of the Conservators for the future can be punctuated by periods of despondency with no apparent cause. Nor can they identify the source of their despair, it is just that their mood takes a downswing and they must ride it out until it lets go of them. In either case—of grave concern about the future on the one hand, or of dampened spirits about the past on the other—it is useless to try to reassure them or cheer them up. The mood will pass in due time.

Responsibility. The basis of self-esteem in Conservators is their dependability. If anything, dependability is their calling card. We cannot wound their self-regard more than by hinting that they are in some way irresponsible and cannot be depended upon. Their pride rests squarely upon a foundation of duties done. Should they, even through accident and through no fault of their own, be found derelict in their duty, then they are subject to a merciless conscience that punishes them with waves of shame. Even dishonesty, much less inability or stupidity, cannot compare as a source of chagrin and embarrassment. They hide their faces on failure of accountability.

Beneficence. Generosity, for Conservators, is virtue itself, while greed originates from demons. Should they give in to some demonic avarice, which ever lurks in their hunger for security, they may feel guilty and so may be guilt ridden even upon being given something or keeping something which they may well deserve. Conservators tend to feel indebted however much they have discharged their debts, as if they were born in debt and never get out of it. This feeling of indebtedness of the Guardians, Conservators and Monitors alike, may well be the source of the doctrine of original sin. Who knows? At any rate, we cannot possibly understand them if we lose sight of the ledger they keep on all their interpersonal relations: each interaction is both debited and credited as something owed and something payed.

Authority. Conservators, more than any other type excepting the Monitors, can put their trust in authority, while they seem unable to trust those who take liberties with the rules or arrogate to themselves rights not duly given them. Who is without proper credentials cannot be counted on, and it is fitting and proper that government agencies see to it that permission is granted only to those passing the scrutiny of those officially sanctioned to license, credential, franchise, and authorize.

Aristocracy. Conservators find in the aristocrat something admirable, something to envy. To be born high, of noble blood, or for that matter, with a silver spoon in one's mouth, would be most salutary. On the other hand they save their disdain and contempt for the barbarian and the uncivilized.

Conventional Consciousness. The Conservators seem to be the ultimate in orthodoxy. They are prone to take the conventions, customs, and traditions of their group very seriously. Things ought to be done in a standard way. Procedures, whenever possible, should conform to the standards set fourth by the group leaders. Opinions approved by established groups are the only ones to hold to firmly. Hypotheses ought to be subjected to the scrutiny of authorities, changes to the tribunals of institutions, rebellion and deviation from the norm summarily punished, especially if the culprit had the wrong attitude. The Conservators' intelligence is mainly associative. Their long suit is in imagining or observing, as the case may be, conventional linkages, associations, and connections. Their thought, in other words, is most effective when it is linear, additive, and correlational. Thus, for example, arithmetic and spelling come more easily to them than, say, the geometries and algebras. Likewise Conservators can be very sensitive to the quantitative. That is, they can be unusually effective in maintaining awareness of matters of degree. This orthodox consciousness, however, does not make them unaware of heterodoxy. Indeed they can be very sensitive to departures from the orthodox, wishing, as they do, to prevent unnecessary change. Prone to maintenance of constancy far more than to analysis of difference, it is sometimes hard for them to address the latter for any length of time. Indeed, the Conservators can devote more time and ability to discerning meanings and implications than to differences and distinctions.

Fatalistic Outlook. As with other kinds of temperament, the Conservators have both positive and negative ways of regarding their surroundings. All Guardians are fatalists in one way or another. It is a matter of fate that things happen the way they do. "Whatever will be, will be," "this is my Karma," "my cup of tea"—each of their sayings speaking of the inevitable, inexorable, and ubiquitous constancies of Mother Nature. On the other hand, in their negative outlook the Conservators are pessimistic. It is well to attend Murphy's Law and heed the warnings of Chicken Little, but it is especially prudent to emulate Aesop's Ant: "Put aside your fiddle, idle Grasshopper, and join me in gathering supplies lest they be covered with snow, leaving all cold and hungry."

SafeKeeping. Conservators are scripted to act out a life of safekeeping, even as children and after retirement. This

scenario shows up at home, at school, at work, at play, and
at community meetings.

Hierarchy. In the home the Conservators, like the Monitor Guardians, establish a place for each member in the
family hierarchy. Autonomy and individualism are not acceptable. Age is due both privilege and respect. The older
siblings have higher status than the younger. And in many
Guardian families, the males are given higher status than
females, though this attitude may have diminished during
the 70s and 80s, especially in the Atlantic and Pacific coastal
cities. All members have specific duties and responsibilities.
They are to do their duties, they are to want to do them, and
they are to want to do them for the proper reason. Dutiful-
ness for the wrong reasons is not acceptable. Conservators
are very protective of their children, even overprotective of
some, in some cases prolonging dependency. As children the
Conservators are responsible, dependable, and dutiful from
infancy. Added to this they usually respect their parents
even when respect is not earned, and are the most likely of
all the types to become rescuers of wayward parents.

Artisan Spouses. Although they can safely marry most
of the types, the Conservators' best bet seems to be the
Artisans, especially the Operators. They alone seem able to
put up with the waywardness of the Operators and are willing to provide anchorage for them and to rescue them from
their escapades. Also they find adventuresomeness of the
Operators appealing and attractive, perhaps because it complements their own caution so well.

Learning Business Operations. At school Conservators, like Monitors, teach and learn business activities
better than the letters, arts, or sciences. Here their orthodox
consciousness and associative and quantitative cognition
give them the edge over others, for most business operations require this sort of intellect. School, especially the

first twelve grades, seems to have been made for the Guardians, the Conservators even more than the Monitors. They wish to please the teacher above all else and never question his or her assignments, method of instruction, intentions, or authority. They are model students, conscientiously following each and every directive, doing all homework, on time, basking in the warmth of the teacher's praise.

Materiel Work. On the job, owing again to their associative and quantitative intellectual talents, Conservators, like Monitors, do best at storage, recording, measurement, retrieval, and dispatching of materiel. In this field they are incomparable, for no other context of work is so well suited to fixed and standardized operations. Clerical work can be very satisfying to them, the brighter ones becoming accountants, bankers, brokers, underwriters, realtors. They have no peers in selling chattel and real properties to those who seek them out for this purpose. You're in good hands with Conservators, for they see to it that they know your needs and meet those needs to your satisfaction.

Indulgent Recreation. At play, insofar as the Conservators take time to play, catering to others and being catered to, is recreational. In a sense, indulging others, even though it is beyond the necessities, is a busman's holiday, and so is not nearly as pleasurable as the luxury of being indulged themselves. While the Artisans are playing games with vigor and abandon, the Idealists are lost in fantasy, and the Rationals are studiously improving their skills, the Guardians, Conservator and Monitor alike, are restfully taking surcease from their obligations as they are passively wined, dined, and amused by entertainers.

Depression. When forced by their lurking fears to behave tactically toward others the Conservators deny their own responsibility by accusing others of abandoning them. Added to this they start up the game of complaining of great burdens and losses that they must countenance and put up with, which reverses have immobilized them. On these complaints they ask to be exempt from their burdens and obligations. Especially they are prone to complain of fears for their health and of feelings of remorse for imaginary derelictions of duty. When such tactics become a nuisance to family and friends the Conservators are referred to by some as Anxious and Melancholic Depressives. Happily, such episodes are usually short lived and tend to give way to an upswing of feeling without interference from others or even situational changes.

Frequency. The Conservators are so nice, so helpful, so considerate, so thoughtful. Fortunately Mother Nature—a Conservator herself—saw fit to supply us with more Conservators than any other type. There may be as many as twenty-five percent of the Caucasian population at any one time, and since these people foster the establishment and maintenance of groups they are the most visible of all the personality types and the easiest to identify. Probably half the families have at least one Conservator parent, and with increasing family size, more than one Conservator offspring. Ordinary classrooms abound in them, to the comfort and delight of the teachers, with perhaps eight in a class of thirty-two in the lower grades, while in the upper grades their percentage is much larger because of the exodus of Artisans from secondary schools.

Providers: **The Gregarious Conservators.** When they feel gregarious the Conservators take up the task of providing others with the necessities of life. The totem deity of the provident Conservators is Vesta, god of hearth and home. Those among the Conservators who are comfortable in their public roles and therefore can approach strangers with ease and confidence are fulfilled in their lives in the degree they can provide others with necessities. They are far and away the best sellers because they are honestly concerned with their customer's welfare and this attitude is quite visible to the buyer. These Providers are talkative. They can chat with anybody about anything that comes into their mind, a sort of free association, bouncing from topic to topic. They remember everybody's name, and the names and particulars of everybody's children and spouse, and everything everybody has been doing. If we wish to know what's been going on in the neighborhood we've but to ask them and they're delighted to tell us all the details. As host or master of ceremonies they are without peer. So gracious, so indefatigable in seeing to it that each is served, so watchful for the isolate, so insistent that all partake of the cornucopia they provide. Here in the gregarious Conservators are the true providers, Santa Claus incarnate, bless their hearts.

Protectors: **The Seclusive Conservators.** Feeling seclusive, Conservators take up the task of protecting others from the pitfalls of life. The totem deity of the protective Conservators is Hera, god of marriage. Those among the Conservators who are not comfortable in their public roles and therefore tend not to approach strangers with ease and confidence are fulfilled in their lives in the degree they can insure the safety of those in their circle. They are far and away the best protectors because they are honestly concerned with their charge's safety, and this attitude is quite visible to those thus sheltered. The harbor, the haven, the sanctuary, the asylum, the castle keep, the sheltering enclosure— this is their arena. Thus it should be no surprise to us that the hospital, and all that transpires in it, is of great significance to the seclusive Conservators. It is not a mere symbol of safety, it is the very substance of safety. The family doctor, rescuer of life and limb; Sara Barton and Florence Nightingale, angels of mercy. And these Protectors go about their business of keeping us safe from harm quietly, without fanfare. They are not talkative like their more gregarious counterparts, the Providers, except with friends and relatives. With the latter, however, they can chat tirelessly, associating freely, in minute detail, for as long as it takes to cover everything concrete in their lives. They are thorough in this as they are in their safety measures. Here in the private and seclusive Conservators are the true and devoted protectors, keeping us out of harm's way; bless them for their vigil.

The Organizers

RoleDirectives. The Organizers[1], more than others prone to issue roledirectives, are the most deliberate and conscious definers of role relationships, and are consequently more likely to take charge than all other types. They do not seek to do so, are not interested in the prestige of command, do not glory in issuing directives. It is just that any enterprise they come upon requires by its very nature that certain outcomes be sought and certain actions be taken to achieve those outcomes. The Organizers *cannot not* see the outcomes and the required actions that are likely to bring them about, thinking always, as they require themselves to do, about the relation between means and ends. Others seem unconcerned on this issue, and their enterprises appear aimless or misdirected to the Organizers, and so they *must* take over to ensure that the goal is reached by the selection, or creation, of appropriate actions. It is this disordered structure

---

[1] Organizers are likely to score high on the N, T, and J scales of the Myers-Briggs Type Indicator and Temperament Sorter, the index of correlation likely to be in the neighborhood of sixty percent (.6).

of reality, both physical and social, that forces them to command.

Efficient Pragmatism. Perhaps the most important thing to know about the Organizers is that they're interested in minimax issues far more than anything else, which is to say, how to bring about the most result for the least effort. Least effort, not because they are lazy—this they could never be—rather because wasted effort bothers them. Their focus is most often on systemics, cybernetics, scientific and technological design. Efficiency is always the issue. Organizers are efficiency pragmatists at all times, everywhere they go, no matter what they do, no matter with whom they interact.

Analogical Pragmatism. But theirs is analogical rather than concrete pragmatics. The model's the thing, for it portrays the contingencies of reality, and contingencies are first, last, and always the important consideration. Too bad for mere reality should it not seem to comport with the Directive Rational's idea of probable sequences. This attitude sometimes appears arrogant, but the arrogance of the Organizer is directed toward natural events, not human desires. The Organizers look upon nature as would sculptors upon a shapeless stone, as raw material to shape into their mindset. Indeed, they are the prime movers who would put their minds to the reshaping of nature itself. If this be arrogance, and many would so regard it, then at least let us distinguish it from vanity, and let us also admit that whoever sculpts nature is the creator of civilization.

ProblemSeeking. The Organizers, like the Engineering Rationals, are far more interested in the theoretical aspect of events than the ethical, aesthetic, or economic. Why me and not you? Why this and not that? Why here and not there? Why now and not later? These debates arise early in life and never cease, to the consternation of parents, teachers, bosses, or officials. The Engineering Rationals, in contrast, may hesitate to pose their incessant questions, preferring to keep the pros and cons inside their own consciousness, but there is no such hesitancy on the part of Organizers. The fuel for these debates is an insatiable curiosity about how things work—though they concentrate fully on one thing at a time—and they continually work on possible solutions for the many problems they collect as they probe into nature. They consider these problems, in whatever domain they arise, of central importance. While they are on the lookout for enigmas and brain twisters, they carefully avoid the trivial and the obvious. For this reason it is difficult for most of them, and for some impossible, to engage in small talk. They simply can't focus on trivialities and usually don't even try. So problem-centered are they that they might be thought of, like the Engineering Rationals, as the Problem Seeking Personality.

Precision. Organizers want to be precise in dealing with problems. Rigorous, exacting, accurate. They don't want to be sloppy or slipshod in the creation or study of paradigms and algorithms—their maps for circumnavigation. They hold that shoddy constructs inevitably lead to error, and it is an unusual Organizer who fails to eschew error. A mistake here and there, now and then, is only to be expected—"the best laid plans of mice and men. . . ." But to make the same mistake twice? No way.

Achievement. At first glance some might mistakenly conclude that these seemingly calm, problem centered, painstakingly accurate mapmakers have no strong needs and are just as phlegmatic in motive as in mood. But beneath the calm exterior is an *intense* longing for achievement and a niggling sense of impending failure. Since they escalate their standard of achievement to fit their latest success, they skate on the edge of failure most of their waking hours. Yesterday's triumph is but today's par. While they only look for problems and would only like to be error free, they *must* achieve, their need perennial and never fully assuaged.

Magic. Insofar as human instincts involve them Organizers are more strongly imprinted with magic than with medicine or hunting, and are not in the least drawn to herding. Thus, they only rarely join groups and are not often found at meetings, or not for long at any rate. This trait is often misunderstood by those of other stamp, the insistence of the Organizers on mastery of the boundaries and coordinates of nature mistaken for arbitrary and hardnosed indifference to others' feelings.

SelfControl. Organizers, like Engineers, would prefer to stay calm—keep their cool, remain unflappable—while others panic and race around nervously and wastefully. As situations heat up, Organizers manage to cool down. They seem able to hold themselves in check by not getting too enthusiastic or excited, and by refusing to worry about matters beyond their control. On the other hand they can get quite intense and pressured about matters that they *can* do something about (and there are few situations they would admit they cannot control). Even so, their emotions are only reluctantly aroused and usually not expressed, such that they're seen as unemotional and phlegmatic.

Ingenuity. Organizers are proud of their ingenuity and do not apologize for holding themselves in high regard. Moreover, they see stupidity on their part as something to be ashamed of. Should they err in some technological venture, they berate themselves unmercifully with such epithets as "turkey," "idiot," "numbskull," and the like. They, like the other Rationals, are highly critical of themselves regarding intelligence, and so do not take kindly to anyone who may make the mistake of criticizing them.

WillPower. While they base their self-esteem on their ingenuity, their sense of virtue rests on the willpower they can muster, and they feel very guilty should that willpower flag. To have resolved that they will, say, diet or quit smoking, and then not to hold to that resolve, they are likely to suffer pangs of guilt. They feel strongly that they *should* do what they said they *would* do.

Reason. Reason is, for Organizers and Engineers alike, their sovereign basis of trust. It is the only thing they'll put their faith in, while they completely distrust anything arbitrary. Many of them, therefore, are predisposed to put logic above all else, and take it for granted that ''if men would but reason together,'' even the most difficult of human difugalties could be untangled.

Genius. They admire the inventive genius above all others, wishing that their own latent genius would someday emerge and flower. Perhaps because their heroes are the geniuses, they selectively develop whatever germs of genius they inherited in their own makeup. But alas, capable as they are of great admiration, they are also capable of great contempt, most of which they reserve for the looter, the secondhander, and the parasite.

Analytic Consciousness. Organizers are analytic. They make distinctions, point out differences, exceptions, absurdities. They are constantly thinking of differences that make a difference, and determining what they regard as the necessary and sufficient conditions under which events occur. Occasionally accused of hairsplitting and nitpicking, they are wont to retort—tongue in cheek—that hairs are to split and nits to pick. This sort of thought, analytic instead of synthetic, differential instead of integral, deductive instead of inductive, comes in two forms: structural analysis and sequential analysis. The Organizers are especially adept at sequential or contingency differentiation, while the other Rationals, the Engineers, are more adept at structural or configurational analysis. Relatively strong in analysis, differentiation, and deduction, they are secondarily strong in synthesis, integration, and induction, the latter natural complements and reciprocals to their strong point. On the other hand both their sense of variation and their sense of convention tend to lag behind. This built-in obliviousness to tradition, orthodoxy, custom, and standard procedure makes some of them seem arrogant, when actually they are only preoccupied with structural and sequential distinctions. This preoccupation with abstract pragmatics makes some of them seem pedantic and even pompous, but this is usually mere illusion, since they are concentrating on their thoughts and not on those with whom they converse.

Relativistic Outlook. In their world perspective the Organizer Rationals are haunted by their inborn solipsism, in which viewpoint all must be seen as relevant only to oneself. Rather frequently they remind themselves that we are all enclosed in an envelope of subjectivity and that we perforce can only imagine the world about and project our own reality upon an indifferent dance of electrons. This may be the basis of their skeptical nature, Organizers and Engineers alike, born skeptics, doubters of assertions by those who have not done their scientific homework. Nothing can be taken for granted, all must be proven, since the way they see it, most images and perceptions are mistaken and riddled with error in spite of good intentions and diligence.

Justice. In the realm of goods and services the major scenario of the Organizers is to insist on justice and fair trading and to demand that all exchanges result in mutual satisfaction to both parties. Organizer types will rarely bargain, will not take advantage of the gullible, and energetically avoid being taken advantage of. They burn for weeks, months, even years when it turns out that they have been hoodwinked. They possess a strong sense of justice and are sometimes outraged when injustice is done. Not surprisingly, revenge, efficiently and poetically executed, is irresistibly attractive to many of them, if only in fantasy.

Individualism. In the family the Organizers, like the other Rationals, insist on unconditional autonomy for all members. They simply will not tolerate the imposition of arbitrary rules for any family member, just as they refuse to tolerate the shielding of an imprudent member from the logical consequences of his or her imprudence. Family members are to be individuals, and treated as such; responsible to themselves alone to develop in their own direction whatever is in them to develop. But they must pay the price should they fail to develop. This does not mean the Organizer, as parent, does not stand ready to assist the child, or spouse for that matter, in reaching for his or her potential. Far from it. It does mean, though, that no one in the family is allowed to evade the logical consequences of dragging heals or putting off the task of development—not in the Organizer's home. As a child member of any family, regardless of the personalities of the parents, the Organizer is autonomous, is an individual to be reckoned with, one who may ignore arbitrary rules, sometimes regardless of the consequences. On the other hand the Organizer as a child is also a born pragmatist and is capable of viewing arbitrary rules as practical necessities, fooling the parent into believing the rules are being obeyed conscientiously.

Idealist Mates. Courting is a special problem for many Rationals, especially the Organizers. That's because selection of a proper mate must be done rationally, but unfortunately the rationale for such action is not usually available. As often as not the Organizers end up with an *impulsive* choice after considerable rumination. Even so, their best bet may be some kind of Idealist. These can appreciate the reasoning capabilities and the strong will of the Organizers while the Organizers reciprocally appreciate them for their romanticism, buoyant enthusiasm, and metaphoric imagination. Of course Organizers can mate with other kinds of personality with some success, but only the Idealist can honestly tell him or her that reason may be useful in technology, but not where feelings enter the scene. Only the Idealists can be irrational and get away with it, while other types must face the Organizer's insistence on being logical and so are usually one down in marital tiffs.

Science and Technology. At school the Organizers are better equipped to teach and learn the scientific and technological than they are letters, arts, or business. They pursue such studies endlessly and efficiently. When they meet with obstacles, such as an inept teacher, or an arbitrary curriculum, the Organizer type student disregards the classroom and takes on the task of self-instruction to develop the intellect. As teachers, they tend to support and facilitate their brightest students, assisting the plodders only with some reluctance, and largely ignoring the disinterested students.

Learning From Others. Organizers do not ignore suggestions by others regarding definition of means and ends. They will listen to anybody who has something to offer, but they will disregard all who do not. The status, prestige, authority, degree, license, credential, badge of office, repute, or manners of the advisor mean absolutely nothing to the Organizers when the issue is pragmatics of goal directed action. They will ignore the saints if their ideas are fruitless and listen to demons should the latter profer fruitful concepts of action. The direction of efficient and effective action toward well defined goals is no place for clowns, even nice ones, or so the Organizers would have it. Organizers promote learning in any manner and degree they can. If knowledge can ensue from observing someone or taking some action, then such is worthwhile; if not, then not.

Strategies. At work the Organizers' interests and abilities lie more in strategy than tactics, personnel, or materiel. Even as subordinates, they insist upon devising strategic or contingency plans for all actions. Perhaps for this reason, in addition to their commanding nature, they tend to rise quickly to positions of control, or to increase the scope of their contractual agreements should they form their own company. They believe, because it is in their nature, that operations not subordinated to goals are inefficient, and goals not subjected to contingency planning are not reached. No self-respecting Organizer would set sail without a chart.

Skills Development. Organizers schedule themselves for rigorous play. If the play is chess, bridge, that sort of thing, there must be continuous improvement, with no backsliding. If the play is tennis, racquetball, or similar activity, all strokes must be put into the repertoire and grooved until errors in execution steadily decline. Perhaps it is an exaggeration to say these people are grim in their recreational activities, but it is no exaggeration to say that they can be rather unhappy with themselves when they fail to eliminate errors. Mind you now, they can play *unhappily*. And it is so much fun for them should they, now and then, turn in a splendid performance! Here are the true skillmongers.

Rationale. Those few Organizers who get involved with community groups such as clubs, churches, and the like, seem more concerned with discussion of rationale than with inspiration or festivity; and they rarely concern themselves with ceremony or ritual. This means that, for instance, even in spiritual matters, they are bent on making sense of things; theology, after all, is logic applied to the stories of the gods, that is to say, the question of coherency of rationale in godly tales.

Obsessions. Everyone uses negative tactics to defend himself or herself sooner or later. Such defense is unconscious and involuntary, puts others at a disadvantage, but is of no apparent advantage to the person so acting. Forced by fears to enact negative tactical maneuvers in relation to others, the Organizers deny responsibility by disqualifying the messages of others, defend themselves by acting as if preoccupied, and increasingly engage others in power struggles. When their tactics become noticeable they are usually called Driven Obsessives and it becomes extremely difficult for others to relate to them. Fortunately, only a small percentage of them are forced to become tactical and even these tend to abandon their maneuvers once they are no longer needed.

Frequency. Since the world doesn't need many chiefs but lots of braves, it is perhaps well that the Organizers comprise a mere five percent of the Caucasian population. Most families are devoid of them and public elementary school classrooms have no more than one, if that. Since they tend to take charge even as children, what others call social skills may be late in coming, and owing to their tendency to keep their own counsel, they're very difficult to spot and hard to get to know.

FieldMarshals: The Gregarious Organizers. When feeling extroverted the Organizers take up the task of marshaling the forces near and far and directing them to remote ends. The genie on their shoulder, which is to say their totem deity, is Atlas, god of world order. The more extroverted, public, and outgoing is the Organizer, the more encompassing his or her marshaling activities. To marshal is to bring into order all within one's field of influence. All. Indeed, so commanding is the demeanor of the extroverted Organizers and so obvious the vision that fuels their advocacy of goal directed action, that most of us do not question or challenge such command; more likely, followers are grateful that someone has the drive and knowledge required for the marshaling of forces.

Planners: The Seclusive Organizers. When seeking privacy the Organizers devise long term contingency plans for launching complex missions aimed at distant goals. They have a genie on their shoulder named Heracles, god of strategy. The more introverted, private, and seclusive are the Organizers, the more inclusive the contingency plans they produce. George Marshall, Dwight Eisenhower, and Ulysses Grant are prototypes. No contingency may be overlooked, no proposed action without a backup. First things first, priorities ruthlessly ordered. Always. But these introverted Organizers must be invited, even persuaded, to take over. They keep their counsel until and unless it is solicited.

The Engineers

RoleInformatives. The Engineers[1] are every bit as logical as their rational counterparts, the Organizers—both aptly called 'Rationals'. Unlike Organizers, however, Engineers will not issue directives without apology, will not define role relationships without a measure of discomfort, will not take charge unless forced to do so by fell circumstance. But they are strongly informative. Let someone tell them of the role they are to play and they will accept or decline the proferred role with very explicit information, and insist upon acknowledgement of the message to boot. In a sense they are neither leaders nor followers, satisfied, as they are, to instruct others on how they are on their way to goals that they alone can envision. They issue RoleInformatives with ease, RoleDirectives with misgivings.

---

[1] Engineers are likely to score high on the N, T, and P scales of the Myers-Briggs Type Indicator and the Temperament Sorter. The index of correlation between the Engineer personality and the two personality tests is probably about sixty percent (.6).

Engineering Pragmatics. Some people feel compelled to make up things, to devise, improvise, or adapt wherever they go and whatever they do. They do not innovate just for kicks, but as a means to certain ends. They have boundless faith in their ingenuity and delight in making models and prototypes of devices and methods never tried before. To the challenge that "it can't be done" their response is, "I can do it." Engineering Rationals are compelled by something inside them to seek those methods, thinking always, as they require themselves to do, on the relation between means and ends. Others seem unconcerned or incompetent on this issue, so the Engineers must, to ensure that the goal is reached, select if available, or devise if not, appropriate tools, materials, and actions. It is the need for—and rarity of—effective means, both physical and social, that sets the stage for the Engineers to innovate.

Analogic Pragmatics. The Engineer types are preoccupied with pragmatics, but pragmatics in the abstract. The model's the thing, for it portrays the relation between structure and function. This relation is the important consideration. Engineers look upon others' reality as almost trivial, a mere arena for testing ideas, and too bad for others' reality should it not comport with the Engineers' definitions and hypotheses. They find all too often that what passes for reality is mere prejudice or convention. This attitude is sometimes criticized as arrogance, the Engineer looking upon nature as no more than raw material to be reshaped according to his or her design. Indeed, the Engineers are the prime designers who would pit their minds against Nature in an endless struggle to wrest from her her immutable laws. If this is arrogance, then at least it is not vanity, and let us admit that whoever harnesses nature is the creator of civilization.

Wordsmanship. The Engineers' abstract attitude is especially noticeable in their precision with speech. Their word arsenal grows through the years and they tend to use it as a tool of debate, arguing on both sides of any issue with equal facility. Few can match their repartee and their quick detection of errors of inclusion, exclusion, or redundancy in others' speech and writing. Those who venture to grapple with them verbally soon find themselves one-down, wondering how it happened so fast. The Engineers also put their verbal skills to use in their attempts to outwit the rules and regulations of the establishment. Prohibit anything, and they will find a legal way around the prohibition. Language is their prime weapon and they wield it like a poniard to pierce the armor of their opponents. They are not so much s*words*men as they are *words*men.

Problems. Engineering types are curious. Like the Organizers, they are far more interested in the theoretical aspect of events than the ethical, aesthetic, or economic. They are curious about many things, finding it hard to concentrate on one thing at a time. They are on the lookout for problems, riddles, enigmas, puzzles. The more complicated the better and they simply ignore the simple and the obvious. For this reason it is difficult for most, and impossible for some, to engage in small talk. They simply can't focus this way and usually don't even try. This preoccupation with problems suggests that they, along with the Organizers, be called the 'Problem Seeking Personality'.

Precision. In their incessant questioning they strive for accuracy and reject errors on their part vehemently. They get after themselves for technological errors with unflattering phrazes such as "idiot," "imbecile," "lunkhead," and "cretinous blockhead." Since Engineers are so self-critical regarding their intellectual powers, they allow no one to criticize them without warrant, and even with warrant, the critic is advised to be cautious and accurate. Just as they hold themselves to be precise, so they require those who essay to remark on their errors to be precise also, at the risk of learning of the precise value the Engineer puts upon their barbs.

Magic. Engineers are more strongly imprinted instinctually with magic than with medicine or hunting, and haven't the slightest interest in herding in any of its human forms. Regarding the latter, they rarely join groups, are not often found at meetings, leave most gatherings shortly after they arrive. These are the would-be wizards. They would *chart* everything, *mark* out the bounderies of all that is known, *define* the limits of all domains of which they are cognizant. This would seem to come naturally to them from their embedded wizardry.

Achievement. Are these apparently calm, questioning, careful mappers as phlegmatic in motive as in mood? Not at all. For behind that tranquil front is a yearning for achievement accompanied by a feeling of lurking failure. Their standards of achievement are adjusted to their highest marks, so they anticipate failure as they strive to succeed. What was progress yesterday is taken for granted today. One must surpass yesterday just to stay even. Engineers may *look for* problems, *like* to be precise, but they *need* to achieve. Achievement is a must and so is not negotiable.

Calmness. As implied above, Engineers prefer to stay calm, to keep their heads when others about them are losing theirs. In heated situations they seem able to hold themselves in check by not getting too enthusiastic or excited and by refusing to worry about matters beyond their control. They are often accused of being cold and uncaring, when in fact they can get quite intense and pressured about matters that they can do something about. They can be as tight as a bowstring when they aren't sure but that there may be something they can do to solve a problem. In general, their emotions are only reluctantly aroused and usually not expressed, so that they're seen as unemotional and impassive.

Ingenuity. Engineers are unabashedly proud of their ingenuity. This does not mean, however, that they brag about it. They may silently pat themselves on the back, but they are just as reluctant to ask for credit for their intellectual products as they are falsely to give credit to others. Credit is a problem for them that they usually are unable to solve. Nonetheless, their self-esteem is based on their feeling of intelligence such that its diminution is a source of embarrassment and chagrin for them.

Reason. The only thing Engineers strongly trust is logical reasoning. They can put some trust in their intuition and some, but less, in their impulses. But they cannot find it within themselves to trust authorities or officials of any kind. Titles, badges, credentials, licenses, uniforms, and the like mean nothing to them so they give them little or no credibility. Logic, on the other hand, is absolute, its laws of exceptionless validity.

Genius. The Engineer's hero is the inventive genius. The prophet is worthy of some admiration, as is the prodigal, but not nearly as much as the genius. The aristocrat, in contrast, is not even given a second glance by the Engineer or by the other Rational, the Organizer. Most Engineers are hero worshipers, tending to choose their heros while still young and hoping to emulate them. Capable of great admiration, they are also capable of great contempt. As in the case of the Organizer Rationals, the Engineers reserve their scathing contempt for the looters, secondhanders, and parasites.

Willpower. Engineers require themselves to keep their will strong. If they will themselves to do something, then they should not let themselves down, volition the source of the Engineer's list of shoulds and oughts. A strong will is their greatest virtue, even more of a virtue than benevolence or bravery or generosity. Weakness of will brings on feelings of guilt much more than lapses of benevolence, bravery, or generosity.

Analytic Consciousness. Engineer types continuously differentiate between things that appear to others to be the same. Their distinctions are usually accurate, and they are quick to point out exceptions, absurdities, solecisms, and non sequiturs in their own and others' positions. They search out those differences that they think make a difference, look for what they believe are the necessary and sufficient conditions for the occurrence of events. Some are regarded as unnecessarily hairsplitting, but they see hairs put on earth for them to split. Their thought—analytic, differential, and deductive instead of synthetic, integral, and inductive—can be both structurally and sequentially analytic. The Engineers, in contrast to the Organizers, are especially given to structural or configurational analysis, while the Organizers are more given to functional or sequential analysis. Relatively effective in both forms of analysis, differentiation, and deduction, they are secondarily effective in synthesis, integration, and induction, the latter natural complements and reciprocals to their strong suit. On the other hand both their sense of change and their sense of maintenance tend to lag behind, especially the latter. Tradition, orthodoxy, custom, and standard procedure escape them, preoccupied as they are with making configurational and sequential distinctions. Their preoccupation with abstract pragmatics—with structure and function—gives observers the impression of pedantry and sometimes even pomposity. But this is usually only illusion, their concentration on their thoughts making them largely unaware of their audience.

Relativistic Outlook. Engineers are solipsists, even if they don't realize it. All is subjective. Reality is projected—there is no thing-in-itself that forces itself upon us—there is no objective reality, we create our world by an act of attribution. Perhaps this built-in subjective relativity is the basis of the Engineers' skeptical nature. For they do have their doubts. They seem to doubt most everything, refusing to take anything for granted. But they are not as concerned about proof and evidence as their cousin Organizers. Indeed, they're prone to make all sorts of assumptions without the slightest intention of checking on them, because they're anxious to get going with their latest design or invention.

Justice. The Rationals, Engineers and Organizers, have a stronger commitment to fair play in interactions than all other types. In the wake of injustice Engineers exercise their fantasy, if not their overt behavior, in engineering the means of setting things right. In trading they will rarely bargain, will not take advantage of the gullible, and guard carefully against being taken advantage of. Some will burn for weeks, months, even years should they allow someone to pull the wool over their eyes. And they are the last to leave revenge, or at least the contemplation thereof, to ethereal beings.

Individualism. The members of the Engineer's family are encouraged to be individualists, regardless of age, gender, or accomplishment. Arbitrary rules for any family member are not tolerated, nor is the shielding of an imprudent member from the logical consequences of his or her imprudence. Family members are responsible to themselves alone to develop in their own direction whatever is in them to develop. They must pay the price for not developing just as they reap the reward for developing. But the Engineer parent stands ready to assist the child, spouse, or grandparent, as the case may be, in reaching for his or her potential. As a child member of any family, regardless of the personalities of the parents, the Engineer is an autonomous individual who usually is able to stand out of harm's way, even though likely to ignore arbitrary rules and evade the consequences of doing so. Engineer children "grow themselves up" and so it is advisable that the parents let them be.

Idealist as Mate. The Engineer's best bet as a mate is the Idealist, for two reasons. First, the Idealist, whether male or female, is very much aware of the Engineer's ingenuity, is highly attracted to it, and very encouraging of it. The latter can bask in the warm glow of Idealist's appreciation. And should the Engineers' many excursions lead to wisdom, then they earn the Idealist's admiration also. Second, the Idealist provides endless mystery for the Engineer with his or her rational nature, so that no matter how long the couple are together the Idealist is forever intriguing, the Engineer never completely fathoming the depths of his or her spouse's personality. Of course Engineers can safely marry some of the other personalities, but such marriages will cost much more in personal adjustment and will require the Engineer to forgo his or her cheering section. On the other hand, it would be something of a mistake to marry either a Monitor or an Operator, neither of whom would appreciate or encourage the unique traits of the Engineer.

Science and Technology. At school the Engineers are better equipped to teach and to learn the sciences than they are letters, arts, or business. They pursue their studies of the sciences endlessly and seemingly randomly, although these apparent excursions have a principled quality known only to the Engineers. They can drop a project of study or production in the middle or even at the beginning, in favor of some other, seemingly unrelated course. But Engineers do not wander; rather, they follow a thread to wherever it takes them in the labyrinth of knowledge. When they meet with obstacles to their investigations, such as a useless teacher, the Engineer student bypasses the teacher and assumes the task of self-instruction as a given in the course of development of intellect. As teachers they tend to support and to facilitate their brightest students, while they assist slower minds only with some reluctance, and will virtually ignore the disinterested student.

Learning From Others. Engineers will listen to any valuable suggestions and will ignore all worthless advice, no matter the status, prestige, authority, degree, license, credential, badge of office, repute, or manners of the advisor. Like Organizers, Engineers will ignore the saints if their ideas on structure or function are fruitless and listen to the devil himself should he offer a fruitful concept of these important issues. But whatever the suggestions, the devising of pragmatic tools and techniques toward well seen goals is the sole province of the Engineers; they are sufficient unto themselves in this, or so they are convinced.

Knowledge. Engineers and Organizers promote learning in any manner and degree they can. If knowledge can ensue from some action, then such action is worthwhile; if not, then not. Engineers are far more interested in the elegance of their inventions than anything else, which is to say, how to engineer the most result for the least effort. Focusing on systemics, cybernetics, scientific and technological architectonics, knowledge of efficiency is always the issue.

Strategy. At work Engineers' interests and abilities lie more in strategy than tactics, personnel, or materiel. They insist upon devising strategic or contingency plans for all actions and in acquiring the means necessary to attain their goal before undertaking any action. They believe, because it is in their nature to do so, that operations not subordinated to goals are inefficient, and goals not subjected to contingency planning are not reached. But the Engineers, in contrast to the Organizers, need only rough sketches and vague planning in order to proceed, relying as they do on ingenuity to get them out of scrapes and pitfalls. Engineers are not noted for thoroughness in preparation and are wont to take off on some enterprise before they've fueled the vehicle or buckled their safety belt. They also tend to lose interest in a problem once they've devised the solution, leaving the details of implementation and clean-up to others they trust. Lastly, Engineers are rather unmindful of time, usually underestimating by a wide margin how long it will take to do something, again their ingenuity making them overconfident.

Skills Development.

At play the verbal fluency of the Engineer often comes out in the form of sardonic wit and play on words. They can be jokers not unlike their Artisan friends, ready to laugh at any who take themselves too seriously. They tend to amass hobbies and to become connoisseurs of beverages or foods or music or gadgets, indeed almost anything that can be appreciated for its nuances of difference. In this they are dilettantes, quite in contrast to their actions at work. But they are like the Organizers in requiring of themselves that they continuously improve in their execution of play activities, whether card games, ball games, or whatever. They may not be as diligent as the Organizers in self-improvement, but the trend is there. Skilled execution is fun, poor execution isn't.

Rationale.

Engineers who get involved with the community groups seem more concerned with rationale than with inspiration or festivity. And they rarely concern themselves with ceremony. For example, this means that even in spiritual matters, such as those found in churches, temples, and synagogues, they still are bent on making sense of things. But in the main Engineers are not much inclined to join groups or go to meetings, and when they do join or attend it is not for long and not with enthusiasm.

Frequency.

Since most people use means instead of inventing them, it may be fortunate that Mother Nature saw fit to give us only enough Engineer types to comprise about five percent of the Caucasian population. Most families are devoid of them and public elementary school classrooms have no more than one or two, if that many. Since they tend to fade into the woodwork as children and quietly observe rather than aggressively participate, what others call social skills may be late in coming. And because they are so self-contained, so lost in their own intellectual world, they are hard for teachers and classmates to get close to.

Obsessions. Sooner or later everybody uses negative tactics to protect himself or herself. In doing so the person involuntarily and unconsciously acts in such a way as to put others in his or her circle at a distinct disadvantage, but what is done seems not to give any advantage to the person so acting. When fears make the Engineers tactical in relation to others, they deny responsibility by disqualifying the messages of others, defend themselves by acting as if preoccupied, and increasingly engage others in power struggles. When their tactics become noticeable they are called Inhibited Obsessives (phobic, aphasic, or both) and it becomes extremely difficult for others to relate to them. Fortunately, only a small percentage of them are forced to become tactical and even these tend to abandon their maneuvers once they are no longer needed.

Inventors: The Gregarious Engineers. When feeling extroverted the Engineers take up the task of inventing whatever is needed to get on with it, and so may be called the 'Inventors'. The Genie on their shoulder and their totem deity is Hermes, god of wizardry. The prototype's the thing, the first gadget of its kind. The more gregarious the Inventor, the more reckless in challenging the establishment and in handling career and financial status.

Designers: The Seclusive Engineers. In seeking privacy the Engineers take up the task of designing, architecting, or defining whatever tools or techniques that are necessary for executing the project at hand, and so may be called 'Designers'. The Genie on their shoulder is named Vulcan, god of design. Design's the thing, the system of coordinates. The more reclusive and private they are, the more cautious are their challenges of the establishment and the more circumspect their management of career and finances.

The Mentors

Idealism. The primary and lifelong focus of the Mentor[1] is on the ontogenesis of persons—evolution and development of themselves and others—through some form of mental influence. Like the Advocates, they are idealistic about growth potential in mankind. Relationships are of prime importance to Mentors and they spontaneously communicate caring for others and a willingness to become involved. They get involved so inadvertently, in fact, that they can become weighted down with too many relationships and too many complicated interpersonal feelings. So sensitive are they to the emotional signals in relationships that they can even feel responsible for the feelings of others, as if they are the emotional transmitter—sometimes to such an extent as to place a burden on the relationship. The Mentors seem able to identify strongly with others, so strongly that they occasionally imitate others without realizing it, over-identifying such as to take on the others' characteristics as

---

[1] Mentors are likely to score high on the N, F, and J scales of the Myers-Briggs Type Indicator and the Temperament Sorter. The index of correlation between the Mentor personality and the two personality tests is probably about sixty percent (.6).

their own. This mimetic overidentification can pose a danger for them and put at risk their own identity. Their incomparable ability to internalize the traits of others can overextend them emotionally and cause them to retreat behind a screen of defensive tactics. No doubt because of this strong ability to identify, people often turn to Mentors for emotional support, sometimes in such degree as to overwhelm them, unable as they are to disconnect themselves easily from others.

RoleDirectives. The Mentors are frequently, if not invariably, proactive, which means they take the initiative in defining role relationships, in most situations making the first move in interpersonal relations, or if responding to another's move, countermanding that move with their own agenda. This is not to say that Mentors are overbearing or openly manipulative; rather, their initiatives are only implied, tacit, embedded in sentiments of social facilitation. Since the Mentors so unwittingly crawl into others' skin and intuit their need to act in a certain manner or direction, it is understandable that they also unwittingly direct others to undertake these actions. Yet so unconscious is the Mentors' directiveness that they are surprised and nonplused when others balk or accuse them of being pushy, since they tend to see themselves as facilitative rather than directive, as catalysts rather than commandants. After all, they but suggest what others need to do, the need of the other the prime consideration.

Cooperation. Thus cooperation—not compliance—is very important in the lives of the Mentor type Idealists, and their ideal is to help people in their circle of influence to be of reciprocal assistance and to discontinue competing, contending, or disputing with each other—fighting in any form is inordinately painful to them and they will do whatever is necessary to avoid it or prevent it. They also cooperate with others in worthy projects and actively seek—even expect—cooperation in their jobs and in their families. At bottom, the Mentor type Idealists dream of perfect interpersonal relationships, raising these relationships to a plane which seldom can sustain the realities of human nature. They seem unable to accept, for long at any rate, that though some of us have hearts of gold we also have feet of clay. This recurrent, if not continuous, belief in ideal relationships can overpower friends, spouse, parent, and offspring, all frequently fallible and sometimes insincere and selfish creatures.

Analogical Communication. The communcations of the Mentor type Idealists are largely symbolic and intuitively interpretive, focusing more on the abstract properties of language than on the audible or visible signals—more on the connotative or suggestive meaning of words than on the denotative, objective "thing itself." Indeed, the concrete, digital, and signal properties of communications easily bore them, since they are so quickly sensitive to nuance, implication, and unconscious meaning. Mentor type Idealists take communications for granted and believe their messages are understood and accepted in the absence of rebuttal. Should they discover somehow (since they do not ask) that they are misunderstood, they are surprised, frustrated, and sometimes hurt. Fortunately they are not often misunderstood or disagreed with, since they are unusually fluent with language, especially with spoken language, though some develop a remarkable written style as well.

Romance. Mentors are far more interested in the ethical side of events than the economic, theoretical, or aesthetic. For example, they are somewhat reluctant to involve themselves in economics, but are not at all reluctant to enlist others in a drive to bolster ethical considerations in economics. After pledging themselves to some individual, group, or cause, they are the most loyal of the types, except perhaps the Advocate Idealists. And their fantasies as well as their favored stories are often excursions into the world of occult powers, influence at a distance, prophetic sensibilia, sympathetic magic. Perhaps this is because they want a little romance in their lives, not all the time, but enough to give spice to life. And they reject the banal and vapid, the bromides of life.

Identity. But more important in understanding the motivation of the Mentor Idealists is their eternal search for personal identity. They consider this search the ethical meaning of their lives, and they cannot really believe that people who disclaim interest in identity really mean it. So pervasive is this search for the real self that the Mentor may aptly be called the Identity Seeking Personality, a personality so many psychologists have written books about. Actually *finding* an identity, however, is a more difficult, perhaps unsolvable problem, involving the Mentors in a paradoxical loss of their sense of reality. Letting the search for self end comfortably (by finally settling on a certain self) can unfortunately feel unreal to the Mentor, as if disloyal to the search. Indeed, it is the sacredness of the search, the loyalty to the mystery of identity, that inspires the Mentor Idealist, not the successful attainment of identity. In this way, having *no* determined identity is the Mentor's identity, and living with this paradox is the Mentor's lifelong burden. For those Mentor types who cannot resolve this paradox, the sense of reality suffers as the price of identity.

Rapport. So, even though they would *like* some romance and *seek* identity, they *hunger* for sympathetic rapport with others, nor can they survive without it. Here is no motive that can be pursued or set aside, willy nilly. This is a thirst that must be assuaged each day, else they wither on the vine. And this ever present need is accompanied by an equally strong aversion to exploitation and callousness on the part of others. Perhaps the strength of this need is related to the strong and early imprinting of the medical instinct in the Idealists, Mentors and Advocates alike, and to the seemingly weak and late imprinting of magic, herding, and hunting, the latter a mere vestige.

Enthusiasm. Most Mentor Idealists are highly emotional in the sense that their emotions are both easily aroused and quickly discharged. They can become very enthusiastic, but they are also easily irritated and at times even irascible. When in a gregarious mood, and owing to their strong drive to recruit others to causes, the Mentors can be astonishingly forceful in exciting followers with their current enthusiasms. But should they be irritated by something they consider wrongful, they can also arouse their followers with their ire.

Authenticity. The self-esteem of the Mentor Idealists rests, as it does with the Advocate types, in the authenticity of their being, and they suffer feelings of shame if they are phony, insincere, or fake. Even a joking reference to their lapses in genuineness may occasion a quick and irate response.

Benevolence. Idealists, Mentors and Advocates, are the most benevolent of all the types. They would be of goodwill to all, even their enemies, suppressing their feelings of enmity as best they can. Because to them benevolence is the greatest virtue, malevolence the greatest vice. Of course generosity and willpower are also virtues to cultivate, but not nearly so much as goodwill. And they do not regard boldness as worth bothering with and forgive cowardice without a second thought.

Feelings. Feeling self-regard in their integrity, feeling virtuous in their benevolence, they can put their trust only in their feelings, while they are wary of their logical inferences, however trustworthy they may seem to others.

The Admirable Prophet. Themselves possessed with some degree of prophetic talent, they admire, and in some cases even revere, the prophet. The prophet, in his or her sagacity regarding the origins and destiny of mankind, serves as a model for them to emulate, in as large a way as possible for them. Not that sages abound to model after, but even though scarce they cannot hide from the probing consciousness of the Mentors. As for contempt, even though they would prefer not to harbor it, nonetheless it is involuntarily called forth when they encounter the bigot with his blind prejudices and abuses.

Metaphoric Expression. The speech of Mentors is replete with what may be called "metaphoric transformations." People and things, alike, are attributed features, facets, properties, and qualities from alien realms. This fellow is a Snake, that one, a Pussy Cat. That car has no gumption. The morning greats us. Yonder telephone pole stands mutely and steadfastly at attention, forever, and carries upon his shoulders the power and messages of a distant world. How splendid a figure! All is animate, and everything is something else. It isn't that this fellow acts *like* a snake, he *is* one, totally, unconditionally. So the analogical cognition of the Mentors governs what they imagine and observe in a manner enabling—or condemning—them to create for themselves a very romantic and even mystical world.

Holistic Consciousness. The consciousness of the Mentors is given to integration, to synthesis, to induction. This does not mean that they deliberately erase distinctions and lines of demarcation. It means only that their consciousness is spontaneously and artlessly panoramic and all-inclusive, occasionally over-inclusive. Thus their consciousness is said to be global and diffuse, and in a sense naive. This holistic, global, diffuse cognition also enables them to spontaneously see or imagine implications, which is to say they are exceptionally sensitive to mere hints, traces, suspicions, suggestions of what lies behind, beneath, above, before, or after what is visible or audible. They seem able to note meaningful details that remain unnoticed to others. This extraordinary sensitivity to suggestion makes the Mentor Idealists the best "mind-readers" by far of all the types. They often seem to know what we're going to say before we say it, or at least after the first word or two. And so quick are they to anticipate messages, that they often complete sentences for speakers, or fill in a word during a pause. In short, the Mentor type Idealists take note of the world with a subtlety that fills even the most mundane object or utterance with profound significance. When William Blake wrote "To see a World in a Grain of Sand," he was unknowingly describing the Idealists, especially the Mentor type. But Mentors can be analytic and deductive too, keenly observing or imagining even minute differences. However they must put their minds to it, for their holism is apt to preempt their consciousness most of the time. Consciousness of the standard or the variable, especially the latter, is not as easy to come by, for both are concrete, and Mentors are probably the least concrete of all the types.

The True Believers. Mentors, like the other kinds of Idealists, are credulous people. They are "the true believers." as Irving Goffman described them so elegantly. They cannot *not* believe that even in the most evil person, there is some redeeming feature: "It's an ill wind indeed that brings no man good." In their world view, then, it is only the good that is real and everlasting, with evil but a passing phase, impermanent, unreal. Even so, the other side of credulity is the strange kind of logic the Idealists, Mentors and Disciples alike, seem to be equipped with, called by some emotional logic, by others, paradoxical logic, by still others, paralogic. This means that in their jaundiced view they see themselves and the world about them paradoxically. Their mission in life is to *have* a mission in life; but it recedes before their attempt to grasp it. They *try* to be spontaneous, and being intentionally spontaneous destroy their spontaneity. They *consciously* seek to be unselfconscious, making themselves all the more selfconscious. They get in *touch* with their feelings and in so doing attenuate them. Their bias, alas, is a Midas touch.

Mutuality. In their home scenario the Mentors care most about mutual consideration among all members of their family, asking that each member, adult or child, male or female, not only care about, but also work to meet the needs of every other member. Mentor type parents expect as a matter of course that their children will look after others in the family—and that they will do so without resentment. If, on those rare occasions, one of the children is a Mentor type, the family soon begins to feel the force of that child's predisposition toward mutual aiding and abetting in the family. The child, in turn, may also feel the sometimes damaging burden of becoming the family diplomat or peacekeeper.

Engineers as Mates. Because of their ability to empathize strongly with others and to encourage development in others, Mentors may mate successfully with any of the personalities, although they face fewer adjustments when they mate with Engineers. The Engineers appreciate *their* appreciation and encouragement, their compassion, and their vivacity; while the Mentors appreciate being needed for something they have in plenty, as well as appreciating the resoluteness, strategic planning, ingenuity, and technological curiosity of the Engineers. All Idealists, Mentors and

Advocates alike, have an enigmatic requirement for their marital relationship, namely that it be *deep and meaningful*. This requirement can be a source of friction unless both spouses are Idealists, because the other types, including the Engineers, don't understand the metaphor, that is, don't see how a relationship can be either 'deep' or 'meaningful'. The Idealists are wise to awaken to this obtuseness of their spouses and realize that persons of other stamp think of containers as deep, messages as meaningful, but relationships as neither.

Learning Letters. School can be where the Mentor's soul abides. School is the place that conduces minds to unfold, and Mentors would take part in that mental conduction. Especially it is there the Mentors are well disposed both to teach and to learn letters more than they are the sciences, arts, or business. Should they, however, opt for the sciences, arts, or even business, they are peerless in teaching these also. But in letters, their global consciousness, metaphoric and implicative imagination and perception make them masters of stories, tales, legends, and myths. The narrative, in any of its forms, is their delight and their strength, their verbal fluency deepening both their pleasure and their ability. They interpret literature so profoundly, and are so easily inspired by it, that they inspire their students, without effort or premeditation. These same characteristics make of them prize students of literature as well as teachers. They not only appreciate the stories they read or hear, but the stylistic details and symbolic motifs of stories loom for them with amazing significance.

Personnel Work. On the job the Mentor type Idealists excel in recruitment, training, deployment, advancement, and counseling of personnel. Their effect on fellow workers is catalytic. Teaching, whether at school or in commerce, comes naturally to them and they automatically reject—or blythly ignore—the well-meant but ill-advised training methods urged upon them by their would-be advisors. They seem to do better as instructors whatever it is they teach, than all other types, owing no doubt to their ability to inspire young and old alike and to enlist them in group participation. Ontogenesis is their domain. The Mentor coach is the charismatic coach, the Mentor literature teacher brims with insight and enthusiasm. The same may be said of counseling, for this too comes to them quite naturally, so willing are they to get personally involved, and so able to divine the nature of client distress. These Idealists shine when they are in charge of the growth and development of new employees, apprentices, students, novices, and clients—anyone with growth potential that can come under the spell of their magic wand.

Make Believe. The favorite form of play for Mentors is fantasy. They are especially adept at this since they practiced doing it so much during childhood. Vicarious experiences through plays, movies, novels, and even daydreaming, is very recreational and even rehabilitative to them.

Inspiration. Mentors attend community groupings more for inspiration than for ceremony, insight, or celebration. In religious groups, for example, as advocates of creeds they are peerless, for the ministry of doctrine is where their metaphoric fluency and integrative consciousness are uniquely employed. They can be spellbinders in this, as have been all great religious leaders both east and west. They are strong supporters of the inspirational function of communal gatherings, whether adult or youth, but the latter have such attraction for them that they often can be found heading them.

Confusion. In starting up negative maneuvers people spontaneously and unwittingly do things that are not advantageous to them, but that put others in their circle at a distinct disadvantage. Such tactics are forced upon them by their fears. Like the Advocates, the Mentors may defend themselves by acting as if confused, they may deny responsibility by ignoring the messages of others, and they may start up blackmail games to gain attention. Finally, when the pressure of the Mentor tactics is sufficient to be felt by others, they are sometimes called Seizure Hysterics, either paralytic, convulsive, or both. Happily, those who go to such lengths to cope with their fears usually do so for only brief periods and then return to normal behavior.

Frequency. There aren't many Mentor Idealists, perhaps five percent of the Caucasoid population, which means they occur only rarely in families and there are only one or two of them in elementary and secondary classrooms. Their frequency increases markedly in certain departments at colleges, especially in the humanities and social sciences. They are not easy to identify since they, like the other Idealists, want to please and while young are very compliant and cooperative.

Pedagogues: The Gregarious Mentors. The Pedagogues seem to pattern themselves after Janus, their totem deity and god of stages of life. Like Janus, they preside over what their followers set out to accomplish. In playing their extroverted role many Mentors can be almost irresistible group leaders. Even as children they may attract a gathering of other children ready to follow them in play or project. They seem able to dream up interesting things for the group to do, without effort or planning, inspired as they are by the responsiveness of their followers. They command without seeming to do so. They expect the very best of those around them, and this expectation, which they present in an encouraging manner, induces action and desire to live up to the expectations. Pedagogues seem to take for granted that their implicit commands will be obeyed, and with good reason, since their suggestions are more often followed than not. In their extroverted role the Mentors are very expressive, even effusive. They do not hesitate to express their feelings, the negative feelings with explosive outbursts or periodic popping off, like a boiling teakettle with a rattling lid, the positive feelings with dramatic and even histrionic flourish. Many of them, with practice, can become spellbinding orators.

Prophets: **The Seclusive Mentors.** In playing their introverted role many of the Mentors, even in childhood, can develop extraordinary use of their imagination. Their totem deity is Aesculapius, god of prophecy, whom they copy, with their uncanny awareness of events in our lives that are yet to occur and of our intents that we ourselves are not yet aware of. Just as it is imprudent to ignore the signs Mother Nature gives us now and then, so it is to ignore the oracle's prophecy. These prophetic ones have the charming characteristic of seeming to take for granted that their prophecies will come to pass—and with good reason, since their prophecies often do foretell the future. They do not hesitate to express their feelings, the negatives with statuesque and mute withdrawal, the positives with quiet and regal acknowledgment. Owing to their quiet benevolence and their keen penetration of our will and intellect, these people do have a kind of regal presence, unmatched by others. They want only the best for us and from us and we cannot help but wish to please them in this.

The Advocates

Romance. The Advocates[1] are in some sense the most idealistic of all the types. Their focus, like that of other Idealists, is on growth potential in each of us, and they want to have a part in the unfolding process that each of us undergoes—their favored metaphor, the butterfly emerging from the cocoon. Maturation is their cause, and somehow their sense of integrity is bound up with this concentration on personal ontogenesis. Their lives are romances, the lifelong issue to remain pure and whole in the face of vicissitudes. Here, in the old age of the Western World, is the Defender of the Faith and the King's Champion of medieval legend.

Cooperation. Advocates are cooperative people, perhaps more than all other personalities. They are so easily distressed by conflict that they will go to any length to resolve

---

[1] Advocates are likely to score high on the N, F, and P scales of the Myers-Briggs Type Indicator and the Temperament Sorter. The index of correlation between the Advocate personality and the two personality tests is probably about sixty percent (.6).

it. Conciliation, pacification, facilitation—these manners of sustaining smooth and productive interactions are near and dear to the heart of every one of them. The Advocates spontaneously identify with others, and are strongly sympathetic to the plight as well as the triumph of others. On occasion their identification with another is so complete that they feel in danger of losing their own identity, and, in times of stress, they may temporarily forget who they are and even experience some disorientation in time and space.

RoleInformatives. Unlike the Mentors, the Advocates are not likely to make the first move in relating to others. They wait patiently and expectantly for others to cast them into productive roles, then educate the rolecaster on their willingness, even delight, in playing the role set for them. Thus they let the roledirector know that they permit and sanction his or her definition of their relationship. Theirs is a sort of reactive and responsive way; they issue role informatives, not role directives. They prefer being seen as loyal followers rather than assertive leaders. In many cases the Advocates center their lives in adapting themselves to the intentions and projects of their chosen leaders. Teachers at all levels of education consider them delightful—and memorable—students, since they respond to all suggestions on what to read, what to report on, what to do (though they may be a little late in their response since they only reluctantly schedule their time). They are especially delightful because they are the most vocal of all the types in appreciating their leaders' intentions, accomplishments, and styles. More than this, they will sometimes attribute unreal powers and abilities to their leaders, making them feel falsely, uncomfortably admired. Advocates are particularly prone to project into others their own ability to see through people; they are quick to believe others can see the flaws in their integrity, can sense their impurities, observe their sinful fantasies. This attribution makes them highly self-conscious, as if on stage parading before their perspicacious leaders. This self-consciousness, ever with them, is for some of them the bane of their existence: impossible to do away with, since they must be conscious of everything, including their appearance in the eyes of others.

Analogical Communication. Advocate type Idealists are very intuitive people, which means that their imagination dominates their observation. It also means that their communications are mainly analogical and symbolic, paying more attention, as they do, to the abstract properties of what they say, write, hear, or read. On the other hand, they must make a special effort to focus on the concrete, indicative, and signal properties of communications. They read between the lines, hear the unspoken message in conversation, are usually looking for hidden meanings and obscure possibilities rather than the actual quantitative and useful attributes of present realities.

Morality. Morality is central in the lives of Advocates. They would do what is good and right. They pledge themselves to the ethical life. Given this commitment to some cause, they are the most loyal of the types. The adoption of a cause, usually early in life, transforms their life into a kind of missionary quest. In some sense they are emissaries, envoys, or disciples. Their loyalties thus harnessed, they are the first to desire a code of ethics for any organization, institution, or enterprise.

Identity. In their causes they seek to know who they are. The search for Self is the ethical meaning of their lives, and so all consuming is this search for their 'true self' that they, along with the Mentors, may aptly be called the Identity Seeking Personality. Many psychologists have written books about this quest for identity. To search for identity is one thing, to find it, quite another. Finding oneself means the

quest is ended and that growth has ceased. Self-definition
is an unending quest, even old age "hath yet its honor and
its toil, something ere the end may yet be done." Having *no*
determinate identity *is* in some sense their identity. But this
is no insoluble paradox for the Advocates as it is for the
Mentors; the Advocates' paradox concerns their integrity,
not their identity.

Rapport. Sympathetic rapport with others is more important to the Advocates than identity and romance. They *need*
it, *hunger* for it. This motive cannot be set aside to fulfill
tomorrow. It must be assuaged each day, else the Advocates
waste away. And this hunger is accompanied by a fierce
aversion to exploitation, whether of them or of other victims. The strength of this need may be related to the strong
and early imprinting of the medical instinct in the Idealists,
Advocates and Mentors alike, and to the seemingly weak
and late imprinting of magic, herding, and hunting, the
latter a mere vestige.

Enthusiasm. Advocates are emotional. Little stimulus is required to arouse their affections and there is no time delay
in their expression. Enthusiasm is their most prevalent
mood and, when feeling gregarious, their expressions of enthusiasm are effusive and contagious. But this mood can be
punctuated with periods of irritability and even irascibility,
though these are quickly over and the current inspiration
returns, to the comfort and appreciation of the Advocate's
family and friends.

Integrity. Integrity is the foundation and seat of the Advocates' self-esteem. Should they violate their own code of
ethics by being phony or fake or sham, they must suffer
shame and may feel like crawling under the nearest rug.
Their need to be genuine at all times and everywhere makes

it very difficult for them to avoid loss of self-esteem, especially since they tend to escalate their standards of authenticity rather than to compromise with life as persons of other make often do. If they were not praised and encouraged as children to be true to themselves and were punished or criticized for their strange ways, then they have problems maintaining high self-esteem as adults. Theirs is a dilemma. Desperate to please on the one hand, yet fiercely guarding their integrity on the other, they must skate on the razor's edge, no easy feat. They can never be sure they are for real because their integrity is more important to them than their sense of reality, integrity surviving at the expense of reality. Their integrity is last to go should life demand of them that they yield up their values.

Benevolence. Idealists, Mentors and Advocates, are the most benevolent of all the types. They even forgive their enemies. Virtue lies in benevolence, and vice in malevolence. They also regard generosity and willpower as virtues, but they do not put them in the same class as goodwill. And boldness, regarded highly by the Artisans, is scarcely worth bothering with, the Advocates regarding cowardice as not in the least a vice.

Intuitiveness. Advocates trust their feelings of right and wrong, good and bad, true and false, useful and useless. Much less do they trust reason and authority, and even less than these, impulse. Logic is OK for some issues; so is authority, but to really be sure, the Advocate waits for that telltale feeling and then he or she knows. Arguments in the face of this are unavailing.

The Revered Sage. Possessed, as they are, with a kind of prophetic awareness—though not as much as the Mentors—the Advocates revere the sagacious prophet more than all others. In his or her sagacity regarding the origins and destiny of mankind, the prophet serves as a model for Advocates. They can also admire genius (insofar as they notice it) and persons of noble birth; but virtuosos, though entertaining, are given no reverence. As for contempt, even though they would prefer not to harbor it, nonetheless it is involuntarily called forth when they encounter the bigot with his blind prejudices and callous abuses.

Holistic Consciousness. The consciousness of the Advocate is integrative. Images and perceptions are spontaneously and artlessly global and diffuse, panoramic and all-inclusive. Advocates don't deliberately erase distinctions, ignore differences, overlook lines of demarcation, it's just that they're usually not interested in them. They fuse and blend otherwise distinct and separate ideas and objects almost effortlessly. Advocates conceive and perceive in transformations. Not always, of course, but much of the time. They endow people and things with qualities and attributes from foreign realms. They say you are an Angel, I, a Demon. A corporation is without morals, a morning without luster, a winter without cheer. Metaphors carry most of the Advocates' messages. It isn't that you act like an Angel, you *are* one. And I don't merely copy some Demon, I *am* one. Hence the metaphoric awareness of the Advocates controls their imagination and observation so to create their own romantic and mysterious environs. Everything is something else, everything is related to everything, and nothing is what it appears to be. This diffuse consciousness makes the Advocates exceptionally reactive to implications, hints, suggestions, hidden meanings, makes them able to read between the lines, see the whole in the part. This extraordinary sensitivity to suggestion enables the Advocate Idealist to be good 'mind readers', though not as good as the Mentors. The Advocates observe and imagine the world about them with a kind of subtlety, attributing significance to even whispers of things largely hidden. Blake's seeing ''a world in a grain of sand" spoke poetically of these Idealists. But their synthetic and inductive awareness does not preclude analysis and deduction, though the latter does not come to them as easily as their abiding global awareness. On the other hand their awareness of customs and conventions is not nearly as vivid, while concentrating on variations and change can be very difficult for them.

True Believers. Advocates are credulous. They see good everywhere; it's an ill wind indeed that brings no man benefit. In their world view, then, it is only the good that is real and permanent, evil but a passing phase, impermanent, unreal.

Paradox. But the other side of credulity is that strange logic called emotional logic, paradoxical logic, or paralogic. Advocates can have a jaundiced view of the world. Like the Mentors, their mission in life is to have a mission in life, thus putting missions just out of reach. They *try* to be spontaneous, and so spontaneity eludes them. They *consciously* avoid selfconsciousness, and so are all the more self-conscious. They wish to be in touch with their feelings, only to lose the very feelings they want to experience more intensely. Midas had it better than they.

Mutuality and Sharing. In the home Advocates insist on reciprocity between all members of their family. This means they would have each member, regardless of age, sex, or ability, show not only concern, but also effort, in meeting the needs of every other member. Very early in their lives children find themselves importuned if not inspired by the Advocate type parent to look after others in the family. As children the Advocates are the most facilitative and overtly caring of the types and tend to be seen by other family members almost as saints.

Organizers as Mates. Because of their ability to identify strongly with others and to encourage development in
others, Advocates may mate successfully with any of the
personalities, although they face fewer adjustments when
they mate with Organizer Rationals. The latter appreciate
them for *their* appreciation and encouragement, for their
compassion, and for their vivacity; the Advocates appreciate being needed for something they have in plenty, as well
as the resoluteness, strategic planning, and technological
curiosity of the Organizers. Advocates, like Mentors, put a
puzzling requirement on their marital relationship: it must
be *deep and meaningful*. This requirement can be a source
of friction unless both spouses are Idealists, because the
other types, Guardians, Artisans, and Rationals, though they
may pretend to, really don't understand this metaphor, that
is, don't see how a relationship can be either 'deep' or
'meaningful'. Those Idealists are wise who note this obtuseness of their spouse and accept it as just one more difference
that adds spice to the relationship. By all means they should
hang on to this requirement, but it is fruitless to expect
others to understand it.

Learning Letters. Advocate type Idealists thrive in school
from kindergarten to graduate studies. School is a very special place for them, a place of metamorphosis, a place where
they can safely awaken from their chrysalis state and unfold. Like the Mentors, they are well disposed to teach and
especially to learn letters far more ably than sciences, arts,
or business. Their metaphoric consciousness, integrative and
implicative imagination and perception conspire to make
them masters of stories, tales, legends, and myths. The narrative, in any of its forms, is their delight and their strength,
their verbal fluency abetting both their pleasure and their
ability. Their love of fiction, combined with their natural
ease of becoming inspired, enables them to inspire their
teachers with their contagious enthusiasm. They not only
appreciate the stories they read or hear, but the style in

which the stories are written is not lost on them. And they, as teachers, as students, or as parents, can easily and with delight make up stories on their own, while most others strain and sweat to grind out a few labored sentences. They are tireless in searching out the details of meaningful stories. They'll dig as deep, go as far, stay as long, and expend as much effort as required to find the truths, whatever the truths they seek may be.

Personnel Work. Advocates are catalysts at work, best in deployment, advancement, counseling, and facilitating in general the activities of other personnel. They shine in one-to-one relating, their verbal fluency and natural effervescence making them quite attractive to fellow employees. They are personal in all their transactions; relationships are never "just business." Indeed it is difficult for them to be businesslike, even when it is necessary. Their effect on others is catalytic, perhaps by contagion, perhaps by imitation. In any event, organizations would do well to have them personalize the enterprises that otherwise drift into dehumanizing bureaucracy and standard operating procedures.

Make Believe. Fantasy and vicarious living is the favorite play mode for Idealists, Advocate and Mentor alike. But Advocates are more likely to indulge themselves in this form of play than Mentors. Since they are not nearly as likely to schedule their time as the more task oriented Mentor, they can get so caught up in their dream world that it may sometimes be difficult for them to come back to the real world. After all, they cannot at once enter the fantasy and also stand by to blow the back-to-work whistle.

Inspirational Grouping. Advocates who become involved in community proceedings are mainly concerned with the inspiration provided by such congregation. As missionaries of religious creeds, for example, they can be zealous, going from person to person bearing the glad tidings. Also it is the religious Advocate who is most likely to seek the cloister in order to meditate and to search the archives for lost or as yet undiscovered inspiration. The reasoning, ceremonies, and especially the festivities that occur in communal groups are not very attractive to Advocates. Meetings must be meaningful, not frivolous bashes with strangers.

Confusion. Should the lives of the Advocates turn awry so much that their fears force them to become tactical in their relatedness with others, they deny responsibility by ignoring the messages of others, they defend themselves by acting as if confused, and they start up games to extort recognition. Finally, during those periods when the pressure of their tactical maneuvers is sufficient to be felt by others, they may be called Amnesic or Delusive Hysterics. Fortunately, most who go to such lengths to protect themselves do so for brief periods only and then return to productive life.

Frequency. The Caucasoid population contains a mere five percent Advocates, which means most nuclear families are without even one, and an ordinary public school elementary classroom may have only one or two of them. Besides being rare, they tend to fit in and get along well with others, so they're not easy for us to spot even when we look for them.

Revealers: The Gregarious Advocates. When they play their extroverted role the Advocates take up the task of unveiling the significant social events that affect our lives. Their totem deity is Pandora, god of disclosure, after whom they seem to have fashioned themselves. The more extroverted, public, and outgoing Revealers are, the more inclined to go everywhere and to look into everything—everywhere and everything, that is to say, when something good or bad is occurring. It is not so much that they are snoopy, though they are sometimes so regarded; rather it is that they can't bear to miss out on what is going on around them. They must know all that is significant for the advance of good and the retreat of evil. They must experience, firsthand, all the important things that are happening. This is why they make good journalists. Heralds of sorts, bearers of tidings, raconteurs, narrators, eager to relate the stories they've uncovered. The strong drive to unveil current events can make them tireless in conversing with others, like fountains that bubble and splash, spilling over their own words to get it all out. The minstrels of old who went from village to village spreading the folklore really haven't changed much aside from acquiring audio and video media.

Healers: The Seclusive Advocates. When feeling seclusive the Advocates take up the task of wholeness and health of self and other. Their totem deity is Hygia, god of health, after whom they seek to fashion themselves. The more introverted, private, seclusive these Healers are, the more inclined to retreat periodically to private places to contemplate the mysteries of life, to examine their virtues and vices, to regain their humility, and in general to recover their threatened wholeness. Many have a subtle, but pervasive, tragic motif threaded through their lives, which comes from their often unhappy childhood. They live a fantasy-filled childhood which, though condoned and even encouraged by a few parents, is discouraged or even punished by most parents. In a literal-minded family, required by their parents to be sociable and industrious in concrete ways, and also given down-to-earth siblings who conform to these parental expectations, such introverted Advocates come to see themselves as ugly ducklings. Other personalities usually shrug off parental expectations that do not fit them, but not the introverted Healers. Wishing to please their parents and siblings, but not knowing quite how to do it, they try to hide their differences, believing they are bad (as their parents often tell them) to be so fanciful, so unlike their more solid brothers and sisters. They wonder, some of them for the rest of their lives, whether they are OK. They are quite OK, just different from the rest of their family—swans reared in a family of ducks. Even so, to realize and really believe this is not easy for them. Some must atone for this evil they have been taught is in them, must somehow sacrifice. With this project of undoing comes a certain fascination with the problem (peculiar to introverted Healers) of good and evil, sacred and profane, pure and sullied, virginal and pregnant. They are drawn toward purity, but they continuously look over their shoulder for the violation that stalks them.

Appendices

Appendix A
A BRIEF TEST OF CHARACTER TRAITS

A questionnaire follows that may help you determine your own character type. You will find instructions for scoring the questionnaire on the page following it. First complete the questionnaire by choosing the one word in each row that best fits you, and circle the letter in front of it. Scoring directions follow the questionnaire.

Appendix B
THE KEIRSEY TEMPERAMENT SORTER

This questionnaire first appeared in the book *Please Understand Me,* by Keirsey and Bates, first published in 1978. It is included here for those who might be interested in comparing the Myers-Briggs terminology with that of Keirsey. Enter your choice of answers (a) or (b) on the answer sheet that follows the test. Directions for scoring follow.

Appendix C
BIBLIOGRAPHY

The bibliography was selected to represent some of the sources that have shaped the author's convictions about the problem of personality, going back to the ancient Greek investigators and forward to those anthropologists, biologists, and sociologists who presented modern system-field theory.

A BRIEF TEST OF CHARACTER TRAITS

Choose the one word in each row that fits you best. If none of them applies to you, then skip that row and go to the next row. Since there are so many little used words in the questionnaire, it may be useful to check some of them in a dictionary.

I prefer to be:	E scemly	Q efficient	Y pleasing	B effective
I prefer feeling:	X inspired	A excited	D concerned	P calm
I take pride in being:	A a winner	D accountable	P competent	X authentic
I'd like being a:	E magnate	Q wizard	Y sage	B prodigal
I'd rather be:	P pragmatic	X ethical	A practical	D traditional
There's virtue in:	Z goodwill	C boldness	F ownership	R independence
I'm confident when:	C dashing	F included	R self-willed	Z in rapport
I most often look for:	X my identity	A adventures	D security	P means
I'm proud of being:	Y genuine	B ahead	E dependable	Q capable
I'm best at:	C expediting	F monitoring	R organizing	Z mentoring
I often crave:	A spontaneity	D ceremony	P achievement	X love
I put my trust in:	D authority	P reason	X intuition	A luck
I am a good:	B crafter	E inspector	Y counselor	Q sequencer
I can be:	B impetuous	E dispirited	Q preoccupied	Y alienated
I'd rather be:	P ingenius	X prophetic	A a prodigy	D dignified
I'm better at:	D logistics	P strategy	X diplomacy	A tactics
I count more on:	B chance	E certification	Q logic	Y instinct
I like being seen as:	R progressive	Z altruistic	C urbane	F forbearing
I'm better acting as:	Z an envoy	C a player	F a broker	R a planner
I tend to be rather:	X credulous	A optimistic	D pessimistic	P skeptical
I'm often:	A cynical	D fatalistic	P solipsistic	X mystical
I often speak in:	B street talk	E polite terms	Q shop talk	Y metaphors
I like myself more if:	D prosperous	P autonomous	X benevolent	A nervy
I often search for:	Q modes	Y Self	B risks	E safety
I like being seen as:	R generative	Z unworldly	C worldly	F dedicated
I have more faith in:	Z feelings	C the breaks	F licensure	R grounds
I often yearn for:	R attainment	Z affection	C whims	F rites
I'm better at:	Q devising	Y championing	B adapting	E supplying
I often want more:	A pleasures	D services	P problems	X romance
I'm more capable in:	Z personalizing	C thematizing	F standardizing	R systemizing
My words are often:	D conventional	P technical	X allegorical	A lingo
Trouble is often:	Y paradoxical	B farcical	E predestined	Q meaningless
I tend to seek:	F immunity	R methodology	Z uniqueness	C gambles
I'm rather often:	Q a doubter	Y a believer	B buoyant	E leery
I often speak:	Z figuratively	C slang	F establishment	R jargon
I'm self-confident if:	P self-directed	X empathic	A impactful	D belonging
I often feel:	Q tranquil	Y enthused	B elated	E serious
I have a hunger for:	Y caring	B impulses	E rituals	Q accomplishment
I often speak of:	P entailment	X cues	A facets	D amounts
Sometimes I get:	Z estranged	C reckless	F downcast	R distracted
I'm better at:	B composing	E insuring	Q configuring	Y conciliating
Bad times are often:	R random	Z inexplicable	C a mockery	F inevitable
Maybe I'll become:	C top dog	F an official	R a mastermind	Z a seer
My best ability is:	D stabilizing	P patterning	X humanizing	A fashioning
I'd be good as:	P a marshaller	X a teacher	A an expediter	D a supervisor
I can do well in:	X advocating	A improvising	D providing	P contriving
I'd like to be:	C a virtuoso	F a magistrate	R a genius	Z an oracle
I prefer to feel:	F solemn	R serene	Z fervent	C thrilled
There's virtue in:	B daring	E affluence	Q independence	Y kindliness
I emphasize:	C description	F evaluation	R definition	Z interpretation
I'm better at:	F providing	R inventing	Z revealing	C performing
I like being seen as:	Y warm	B sophisticated	E staunch	Q productive
I'm confident if I'm:	E a member	Q strong-willed	Y sympathetic	B impressive
I like myself if I'm:	R skilled	Z sincere	C competitive	F responsible
Under stress I can get:	D depressed	P preoccupied	X confused	A impulsive

© David Keirsey

Directions for scoring:

Determine your score by adding together the number of A, B, and C choices, then the D, E, and F choices, then the P, Q, and R, and finally the X, Y, and Z choices. The largest of these sums indicates which of the four temperaments you are probably most like.

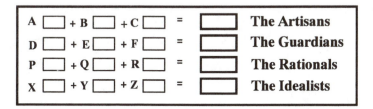

The Keirsey Temperament Sorter

1 At a party do you
   (a) interact with many, including strangers
   (b) interact with a few, known to you

2 Are you more
   (a) realistic   (b) philosophically inclined

3 Are you more intrigued by
   (a) facts   (b) similes

4 Are you usually more
   (a) fair minded   (b) kind hearted

5 Do you tend to be more
   (a) dispassionate   (b) sympathetic

6 Do you prefer to work
   (a) to deadlines   (b) just "whenever"

7 Do you tend to choose
   (a) rather carefully   (b) somewhat impulsively

8 At parties do you
   (a) stay late, with increasing energy
   (b) leave early, with decreased energy

9 Are you a more
   (a) sensible person   (b) reflective person

10 Are you more drawn to
   (a) hard data   (b) abstruse ideas

11 Is it more natural for you to be
   (a) fair to others   (b) nice to others

   12 In first approaching others are you more
   (a) impersonal and detached   (b) personal and engaging

13 Are you usually more
   (a) punctual   (b) leisurely

14 Does it bother you more having things
   (a) incomplete   (b) completed

15 In your social groups do you
   (a) keep abreast of others' happenings
   (b) get behind on the news

16 Are you usually more interested in
   (a) specifics   (b) concepts

17 Do you prefer writers who
   (a) say what they mean   (b) use lots of analogies

18 Are you more naturally
   (a) impartial   (b) compassionate

19 In judging are you more likely to be
   (a) impersonal   (b) sentimental

20 Do you usually
   (a) settle things   (b) keep options open

21 Are you usually rather
   (a) quick to agree to a time   (b) reluctant to agree to a time

22 In phoning do you
   (a) just start talking   (b) rehearse what you'll say

23 Facts
   (a) speak for themselves   (b) usually require interpretation

24 Do you prefer to work with
   (a) practical information   (b) abstract ideas

25 Are you inclined to be more
   (a) cool headed   (b) warm hearted

26 Would you rather be
   (a) more just than merciful   (b) more merciful than just

27 Are you more comfortable
   (a) setting a schedule   (b) putting things off

28 Are you more comfortable with
   (a) written agreements   (b) handshake agreements

29 In company do you
   (a) start conversations   (b) wait to be approached

30 Traditional common sense is
   (a) usually trustworthy   (b) often misleading

31 Children often do not
   (a) make themselves useful enough   (b) daydream enough

32 Are you usually more
   (a) tough minded   (b) tender hearted

33 Are you more
   (a) firm than gentle   (b) gentle than firm

34 Are you more prone to keep things
   (a) well organized   (b) open-ended

35 Do you put more value on the
   (a) definite   (b) variable

36 Does new interaction with others
   (a) stimulate and energize you   (b) tax your reserves

   37 Are you more frequently
   (a) a practical sort of person   (b) an abstract sort of person

38 Which are you drawn to
   (a) accurate perception   (b) concept formation

39 Which is more satisfying
   (a) to discuss an issue thoroughly
   (b) to arrive at agreement on an issue

40 Which rules you more:
   (a) your head   (b) your heart

41 Are you more comfortable with work
   (a) contracted   (b) done on a casual basis

42 Do you prefer things to be
   (a) neat and orderly   (b) optional

43 Do you prefer
   (a) many friends with brief contact
   (b) a few friends with longer contact

44 Are you more drawn to
(a) substantial information   (b) credible assumptions

45 Are you more interested in
(a) production   (b) research

46 Are you more comfortable when you are
(a) objective   (b) personal

47 Do you value in yourself more that you are
(a) unwavering   (b) devoted

48 Are you more comfortable with
(a) final statements   (b) tentative statements

49 Are you more comfortable
(a) after a decision   (b) before a decision

50 Do you
(a) speak easily and at length with strangers
(b) find little to say to strangers

51 Are you usually more interested in the
(a) particular instance   (b) general case

52 Do you feel
(a) more practical than ingenious   (b) more ingenious than practical

53 Are you typically more a person of
(a) clear reason   (b) strong feeling

54 Are you inclined more to be
(a) fair-minded   (b) sympathetic

55 Is it preferable mostly to
(a) make sure things are arranged   (b) just let things happen

56 Is it your way more to
(a) get things settled   (b) put off settlement

57 When the phone rings do you
(a) hasten to get to it first   (b) hope someone else will answer

58 Do you prize more in yourself a
    (a) good sense of reality   (b) good imagination

59 Are you drawn more to
    (a) fundamentals   (b) overtones

60 In judging are you more usually more
    (a) neutral   (b) charitable

61 Do you consider yourself more
    (a) clear headed   (b) good willed

62 Are you more prone to
    (a) schedule events   (b) take things as they come

63 Are you a person that is more
    (a) routinized   (b) whimsical

64 Are you more inclined to be
    (a) easy to approach   (b) somewhat reserved

65 Do you have more fun with
    (a) hands-on experience   (b) blue sky fantasy

66 In writings do you prefer
    (a) the more literal   (b) the more figurative

67 Are you usually more
    (a) unbiased   (b) compassionate

68 Are you typically more
    (a) just than lenient   (b) lenient than just

69 Is it more like you to
    (a) make snap judgments   (b) delay making judgements

70 Do you tend to be more
    (a) deliberate than spontaneous   (b) spontaneous than deliberate

Answer Sheet

Enter a check for each answer in the column for **a** or **b**

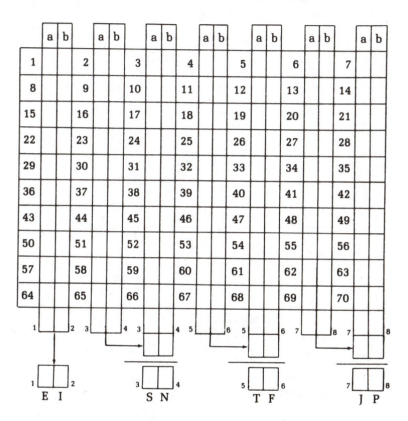

Directions for Scoring

1. Add down so that the total number of "a" answers is written in the box at the bottom of each column (see next page for illustration). Do the same for the "b" answers you have checked. Each of the 14 boxes should have a number in it.

2. Transfer the number in box No. 1 of the answer sheet to box No. 1 below the answer sheet. Do this for box No. 2 as well. Note, however, that you have two numbers for boxes 3 through 8. Bring down the first number for each box beneath the second, as indicated by the arrows. Now add all the pairs of numbers and enter the total in the boxes below the answer sheet, so each box has only one number.

3. Now you have four pairs of numbers. Circle the letter below the larger number of each pair (see answer sheet below for illustration). If the two numbers of any pair are equal, then circle neither, but put a large X below them and circle it.

#	a	b	#	a	b	#	a	b	#	a	b	#	a	b	#	a	b	#	a	b
1	✓		2	✓		3	✓		4		✓	5		✓	6	✓		7		✓
8	✓		9	✓		10	✓		11		✓	12		✓	13	✓		14	✓	
15	✓		16	✓		17	✓		18		✓	19		✓	20	✓		21	✓	
22		✓	23	✓		24	✓		25		✓	26		✓	27	✓		28	✓	
29	✓		30	✓		31		✓	32		✓	33		✓	34	✓		35	✓	
36	✓		37	✓		38	✓		39		✓	40		✓	41	✓		42	✓	
43		✓	44		✓	45	✓		46		✓	47		✓	48	✓		49		✓
50	✓		51	✓		52	✓		53		✓	54	✓		55	✓		56	✓	
57	✓		58	✓		59	✓		60		✓	61		✓	62	✓		63		✓
64	✓		65	✓		66		✓	67		✓	68		✓	69	✓		70	✓	

1 **8 2** 2 3 **9 1** 4 3 **8 2** 4 5 **0 10** 6 5 **1 9** 6 7 **10 0** 8 7 **1 3** 8

→ **9 1**   → **0 10**   → **10 0**

1 **8 2** 2   3 **17 3** 4   5 **1 19** 6   7 **17 3** 8

Ⓔ I   Ⓢ N   T Ⓕ   Ⓟ P

You have now identified your "type." It should be one of the following:

INFP	ISFP	INTP	ISTP
ENFP	ESFP	ENTP	ESTP
INFJ	ISFJ	INTJ	ISTJ
ENFJ	ESFJ	ENTJ	ESTJ

Bibliography

Adams, P. 1973	*Obsessive Children*
Adickes, E. 1907	*Character und Weltanschauung*
Alexander, F. 1948	*Studies in Psychosomatic Medicine*
Angyal, A. 1965	*Neurosis and Treatment*
Ansbacher, H. 1956	*The Individual Psychology of Alfred Adler*
Bertalanffy, L. 1933	*Modern Theories of Development*
Blanshard, B. 1939	*The Nature of Thought*
Buhler, K. 1924	*The Mental Development of Children*
Cassirer, E. 1945	*Language and Myth*
Cassirer, E. 1948	*An Essay on Man*
Cassirer, E. 1950	*The Problem of Knowledge*
Cassirer, E. 1955	*The Philosophy of Symbolic Forms*
Child, C. 1924	*Physiological Foundations of Behavior*
Christie, 1970	*Studies in Machiavellianism*
Cleckley, H. 1964	*The Mask of Sanity*
Coghill, G. 1929	*Anatomy and the Problem of Behavior*
Frazer, J. 1918	*Folklore in the Old Testament*
Frazer, J. 1922	*The Golden Bough*
Fromm, E. 1947	*Man for Himself*
Goldstein, K. 1939	*The Organism*
Goldstein, K. 1947	*Human Nature*
Goldstein, K. 1948	*Language and Language Disorders*
Gurwitsch, A. 1964	*The Field of Consciousness*
Haldane, J. 1919	*The New Physiology and Other Addresses*
Haley, J. 1963	*Strategies of Psychotherapy*
Haley, J. 1969	*Power Tactics of Jesus Christ*
Haley, J. 1981	*Reflections on Therapy*
Haley, J. 1986	*Conversations with Milton Erickson*
Hippocrates 450 BC	*Human Nature*
Hunt, J. 1944	*Personality and the Behavior Disorders*
Janet, P. 1903	*Obsessions and Psychasthenia*

Janet, P. 1907   *The Major Symptoms of Hysteria*
Jung, C. 1920   *Psychological Types*
Keirsey, D. 1967   *The Polarization of Intelligence*
Keirsey, D. 1978   *Please Understand Me*
Kipnis, D. 1971   *Character Structure and Impulsiveness*
Koffka, K. 1924   *Growth of the Mind*
Koffka, K. 1935   *Principles of Gestalt Psychology*
Köhler, W. 1947   *Gestalt Psychology*
Köhler, W. 1938   *The Place of Value in a World of Facts*
Kretschmer, E. 1920   *Physique and Character*
Kretschmer, E. 1931   *Psychology of Men of Genius*
Kretschmer, E. 1960   *Hysteria, Reflex and Instinct*
Lewin, K. 1935   *A Dynamic Theory of Personality*
Maslow, A. 1954   *Motivation and Personality*
Merleau-Ponty 1942   *The Structure of Behavior*
Merleau-Ponty 1962   *The Phenomenology of Perception*
Myers, I. 1962   *The Myers-Briggs Type Indicator*
Myers, I. 1980   *Gifts Differing*
Paracelsus 1550   *Nymphs, Gnomes, Sylphs and Salamanders*

Reusch, J. 1950   *Disorders of Communication*
Roback, A. 1927   *The Psychology of Character*
Sainsbury, G. 1927   *The Theory of Polarity*
Shapiro, D. 1965   *Neurotic Styles*
Sheldon, W. 1942   *Varieties of Temperament*
Sheldon, W. 1949   *Varieties of Delinquent Youth*
Sheldon, W. 1954   *Atlas of Men*
Spränger. E. 1920   *Types of Men*
Straus, E. 1948   *On Obsession*
Strauss, E. 1963   *The Primary World of the Senses*
Sullivan, H. 1956   *Clinical Studies in Psychiatry*
Sullivan, H. 1972   *Personal Psychopathology*
Uexküll, J. 1909   *Umwelt und Innenwelt der Tiere*
Uexküll, J. 1928   *Theoretische Biologie*
Ungerer, E. 1926   *Die Regulationen der Pflantzen*
Vieth, I. 1965   *Hysteria*
Wertheimer, M. 1954   *Productive Thinking*
Wheeler, R. 1929   *The Science of Psychology*
Wheeler, R. 1933   *The Principles of Mental Development*
Wheeler, R. 1934   *The Laws of Human Nature*
Wiener, N. 1950   *Cybernetics*

PROMETHEUS NEMESIS BOOKS
ORDER FORM

Please Understand Me Keirsey & Bates   208 pages—$11.95
National Best Seller. Over 1.5 million copies sold. A 40 year clinical study of differences in temperament and character in mating, parenting, teaching, and leading. Defines four types: Dionysians (SP), Epimethians (SJ), Prometheans (NT), & Apollonians (NF). *Keirsey Temperament Sorter* included.

Please Understand Me, The Videotape   40 Minutes—$14.95
Displays many of the character traits of the NF "Idealist," NT "Rational," SJ "Guardian," and SP "Artisan." Shows the impact of attitudes and habits of temperament and character in mating, management, and education.

Please Understand Me, The Audiotape   6 Tapes—$29.95

The Sixteen Types Keirsey   48 pages—$3.00
Reprinted from *Please Understand Me.* Plus *The Keirsey Temperament Sorter.*

Individual Portraits of the Sixteen Types —specify number of each @ $.20
___ESTJ ___ISTJ ___ESFJ ___ISFJ ___ESTP ___ISTP ___ESFP ___ISFP
___ENTJ ___INTJ ___ENFJ ___INFJ ___ENTP ___INTP ___ENFP ___INFP

Temperament in Leading Keirsey   48 pages—$ 3.00
An essay on differing styles of results management depending on temperament and character. Used by many very large corporations to train management in production, distribution, and personnel recruitment, training, and deployment. Includes *The Keirsey Temperament Sorter.*

The Keirsey Temperament Sorter $.25
A self-scoring test to identify sixteen variants of the four temperaments, reprinted from *Please Understand Me.* Number one best selling personality inventory in America.

The Keirsey Temperament Sorter on Disc $9.95
Self-scoring test to identify 16 variants of the four temperaments. Includes the 16 portraits of temperament reprinted from *Please Understand Me.* Specify Macintosh (Hypercard) or IBM.

Por Favor Compréndeme Keirsey & Bates   238 pages—$11.95
Spanish edition of *Please Understand Me.* Includes *The Keirsey Temperament Sorter* in Spanish.

El Keirsey Temperamento Determinente $.25
Spanish translation of the Keirsey Temperament Sorter, reprinted from *Por Favor Comprendeme.*

Versteh Mich Bitte Keirsey & Bates   276 pages—$11.95
German edition of *Please Understand Me.* Includes *The Keirsey Temperament Sorter* in German.

Presidential Temperament Keirsey, Choiniere   610 pages—$9.95
Depicts the temperament-determined characters of forty U.S. presidents, from youth to old age. Authors found 20 Guardians [SJ], 12 Artisans [SP], 8 Rationals [NT], and *no* Idealists [NF]. Temperament is shown to dominate temporal and regional circumstances and situations in determining presidential behavior—in war and peace—in depressed and prosperous economics—in foreign and domestic politics.

Portraits of Temperament Keirsey   124 pages—$9.95
The four Keirseyan temperaments are named Artisan, Guardian, Rational, and Idealist, each with two variant patterns of behavior based on differing kinds of ability and interest.

A Brief Test of Character Traits Keirsey $.25
Shows four types of temperament and character: Artisan SPs, Rational NTs, Guardian SJs, & Idealist NFs. Reprint from *Portraits of Temperament.*

Qty $0.00

The Pygmalion Project: 1 The Artisan Montgomery   180 pages—$9.95
The Artisan [SP] style of relating to Guardian [SJ], Rational [NT], and Idealist
[NF] mates, shown by characters in novels, plays, and films, such as D. H.
Lawrence's *Lady Chatterly's Lover*, Ernest Hemingway's *The Sun Also Rises*,
and Sinclair Lewis's *The Great Gatsby*, and others.
The Pygmalion Project: 2 The Guardian Montgomery   258 pages—$9.95
The Guardian [SJ] style of relating to Artisan [SP], Rational [NT], and Idealist
[NF] mates, as shown by characters in novels, plays, and films, such as C.S.
Forester's *African Queen*, Jane Austen's *Pride and Prejudice*, Henrik Ibsen's *A
Doll House*, and others.
The Pygmalion Project: 3 The Idealist Montgomery   325 pages—$9.95
A careful and imaginative study of how Idealists [NF] relate to their Artisan
[SP], Guardian [SJ], and Rational [NT] mates, as illustrated by characters in
novels and films such as Forster's *Howards End*, Tolstoy's *Anna Karenina*,
Brontë's *Jane Eyre*, and others.
Children The Challenge Dreikurs, Soltz   335 pages—$11.00
There is no substitute for this manual for those parents, teachers, and counselors
who wish to establish and maintain cooperative and productive relations with
children.
Talk So Kids Will Listen and Listen So Kids Will Talk   242 pages—$10.00
The authors, Mazlish and Faber, teach parents, teachers, and counselors who
wish to learn the gentle art of talking with children effectively and with mutual
respect, how to do it.
Abuse it—Lose it Keirsey   20 pages—$2.00
Applies the principle of logical consequences and the abuse it—lose it method
for developing self-control in mischievous school boys stigmatized as cases of
"attention deficit disorder" and then drugged into obedience with cocaine-like
narcotics.
Drugged Obedience in the School Keirsey   8 pages—$.25
A comparison between drugging mischievous school boys with cocaine-like
narcotics, and the abuse it—lose it method of teaching self-control to these same
children while keeping them in school.
Toxic Psychiatry Breggin   464 pages—$24.95
Dr. Breggin, a noted psychiatrist, 1) unveils the increasing takeover of
psychiatry by drug manufacturers in the promotion of behavior-control drugs;
2) reveals suppressed reports demonstrating the"lobotomizing" effect of
behavior-control drugs; 3) reveals that cocaine-like drugs are being given to one
million school children yearly to suppress them, often resulting in addiction,
loss of muscle control, insomnia, growth suppression, and damaged self-image.